CHURCH
FOR THE
UNCHURCHED

CHURCH
FOR THE
UNCHURCHED

George G. Hunter III

Abingdon Press
Nashville

CHURCH FOR THE UNCHURCHED

Copyright © 1996 by Abingdon Press

This book is printed on recycled, acid-free paper.

Library of Congress Cataloging-in-Publication Data

Hunter, George G.
    Church for the unchurched : the rebirth of "apostolic congregations" across the American mission field / George G. Hunter III.
       p.   cm.
    Includes bibliographical references and index.
    ISBN 0-687-27732-9 (pbk. : alk. paper)
    1. Church growth. 2. Evangelistic work. I. Title.
BV652.25.H838 1996
253—dc20   95-44511
                                                                CIP

Except for brief paraphrases or unless otherwise indicated, scripture quotations are from the New Revised Standard Version Bible, copyright © 1989, by the Division of Christian Education of the National Council of the Churches of Christ in the United States of America.

Those noted NIV are taken from the *Holy Bible: New International Version.* Copyright © 1973, 1978, 1984, by the International Bible Society. Used by permission of Zondervan Bible Publishers.

Theme from "Cheers" ("Where Everybody Knows Your Name"); Gary Portnoy and Judy Hart Angelo. Copyright © 1982 by Addax Music Co. Inc.

97 98 99 00 01 02 03 04 05—10 9 8 7 6 5 4

MANUFACTURED IN THE UNITED STATES OF AMERICA

With love and appreciation to the three generations of
life-affirming, devoted women in my life—

Barbara Craig Hunter

Ella Fay Price Hunter

Monica Mistelle Hunter

Contents

Foreword

This book calls for revolution—the revolution that must take place if the churches in America are to thrive and to fulfill the Great Commission. *Church for the Unchurched* is about the "abolition" of the laity.

God's dream for his church from the earliest time has been that we practice the priesthood of all believers, that we be a kingdom of priests (Exodus 19:6). In its first 300 years of history, the church had no clergy. Rather, it was made up of believers who understood they were to be apostles, sent on mission by the living Christ. With the phenomenal growth of that early church, both numerically and in influence, two classes of Christians emerged, leaders and spectators. The spectators were supposed to learn sound doctrine, to pray, sing, listen to sermons, and pay the bills. But when the question is asked, as it often is, "Why doesn't the church do something about . . . ," "the church" is synonymous with "the clergy."

I believe the two most significant books about the church to be published in this decade are both by George Hunter. His first book, *How to Reach Secular People,* outlined a historical precedent for being an apostolic church. This second book, *Church for the Unchurched,* tells us how. It studies a number of apostolic congregations from various traditions and assorted geographical locations that are successfully reaching the unchurched. It is full of recipes that any serious congregation could copy and use. I wish it were in my power to buy copies of both of these books to give to every believer, to every elder, deacon, vestryman, pastor, or bishop. That could result in a Copernican revolution in the church—the empowerment of the laity.

Matt Williams, third baseman for the San Francisco Giants, said recently, "Baseball is a wonderful game to play. But, frankly, if I wasn't playing, I wouldn't watch it. It's too boring." In a *Newsweek* feature story on the reason for the decline of churches, the bottom line was that people find church boring. George Hunter has been researching those places where church is anything but boring.

He reports on some of the powerful concepts that are shaping the growing churches in our time. One is to use the term "pre-Christian" for all those we have been calling "unchurched" or secular or sinners or agnostics or atheists. That positive mind-set is an important key in evangelism. Another growing church stresses that the people are the ministers and the pastors are the administrators. The pastor explains it this way, "The staff make most of the necessary administrative decisions, thus freeing the laity from the consuming involvements that immobilize, divide, and exhaust most congregations, thereby freeing the people's time and energy for ministry and outreach in the community." The goal for that church is to turn an audience into an army.

One church I know makes the point with a sign at the place where their parking lot ends and the highway begins. The sign says, "You are now entering the mission field." Amen. Let's remember, Jesus did not tell the world to go to church. He told the church to go to the world.

I urge you not only to read this book by this researcher-prophet, but also to apply his message to your own situation. Empowerment is available to all of God's people (Acts 1:8). We are not in a post-Christian era. We are in a pre-Christian era. Most of our churches don't need renewal, they need "newal."

When the marketplace, not the sanctuary, is the playing field, when the laity are apostolic agents, and when we are empowered by the Holy Spirit, we are on the threshold of a great tomorrow.

Bruce Larson
Minister-at-Large, Crystal Cathedral

Preface

Old Trinity Church's membership and attendance had declined for a quarter century. More recently, their finances began declining, the organ needed renovation, there were staff turnovers and then staff cutbacks, and low morale now hounded the remaining members. Meanwhile, a survey of the voting precincts in Trinity Church's ministry area revealed that over 60 percent of the people were unchurched, and over 40 percent had never been church members. Pastor Bob, in a meeting with Helen (Trinity's board chair) and Jack (Trinity's trustees chair) asked, "How can our membership be declining when we are surrounded by so many unchurched people?" Jack suggested that "maybe those folks don't go in for religion. Maybe they aren't the type. They seldom visit our church, and the few who visit don't come back. They didn't even attend our Lenten Preaching Mission last year. Besides, most of the other mainline churches in town have declined about like us."

"Maybe," Helen conceded, "but Community Church down the street has grown a whole lot, and most of the people who join there were unchurched. They don't even have an organ or a choir or hymnals, and I hear that their lay people do most of the ministry; yet they have to schedule three Sunday morning services to handle their crowds. If Community Church can reach unchurched people, why can't we, and why can't the other churches?" Jack replied: "But some of those unchurched people have no idea what we believe or value! If fifty of them came, and wanted to join, what would we do with them?"

The leaders of Old Trinity Church have experienced their local version of a profound change that has taken place in the relationship between traditional churches and the growing numbers of "secular people" across North America who do not know what the churches are talking about. In

11

most communities, most traditional churches cannot reach, or even meaningfully converse with, their unchurched non-Christian neighbors. In most communities, churches can no longer graft a "good evangelism program" onto a traditional congregation and expect much to happen. Most traditional churches, despite the loyalty and devotion of their people and the conscientiousness of their clergy, can no longer evangelize their communities, and many churches cannot even retain most of their own young people.

Meanwhile, in this same generation, we observe the rise and spread of a distinctive type of church that I call the "apostolic" congregation. In various cultural forms, apostolic congregations have existed since early in the Christian movement, and they are prominent in many Third World fields of mission today. This breed of church was reborn in the U.S. in the 1970s, began spreading in the 1980s, and is now found in virtually every city in North America in the 1990s. While several of these churches are better known than the others, there are now hundreds of apostolic churches across North America, and we can expect thousands of them by the early twenty-first century.

These churches are very different from the two types of traditional churches that predominate, and usually stagnate, across North America. These two types are: (1) The traditional evangelical churches that perpetuate the forms of evangelicalism that flourished in the nineteenth century, and (2) The traditional liberal churches that perpetuate early twentieth century patterns that thrived as late as the 1950s.

On the surface, there are four obvious ways in which the new apostolic congregations are different from the two types of traditional congregations. First, apostolic churches are reaching significant numbers of the unchurched, non-Christian, secular people in America's mission fields. (Indeed, that is their main business.) Second, they employ the language, music, and so on of the people they are called to reach, rather than their tradition's language, music, and so on. Third, they are on the edge of their denomination (or they have no denominational attachment at all). Fourth, both the conservative and the liberal Protestant establishments are anxious about the new apostolic congregations; they are often quick to criticize, yet they envy their capacity to reach unchurched pre-Christian people.

Almost anyone who visits an apostolic church senses that they are different from the two traditional types of churches. This project probes beneath the surface to stake out the essential differences that make it possible for apostolic churches to reach a secular unchurched population. Leaders of traditional churches may want to take these differences seriously, because it is possible for conventional churches to move from tradition to mission!

To be sure, today's apostolic churches are not all alike, any more than the churches of the New Testament period were all alike; indeed, one finds enough variety among them to find an exception to almost any generalization. Nevertheless, they share some common features, and those features contribute to their strength and contagion. With the background of reflecting for thirty years upon the challenge of reaching secular people, this project took me to nine apostolic congregations in which I did some field research. I identified the churches to research using the following criteria:

• I identified churches whose mission is to be a mission to unchurched pre-Christian people.
• I identified churches whose growth is substantially due to strategic principles and directions that are reproducible in other churches.
• I eliminated churches whose growth among the target population was primarily due to the charisma of the senior pastor, since such people are not reproducible.
• I eliminated several churches that emphasize "prosperity gospel" or "patriotic Christianity."
• I identified churches that had essentially invented their "apostolic act" themselves.
• Limited time and travel budget prevented me from researching more churches that looked promising, but by now I was meeting the same principles over and over, and telephone conversations with leaders of some of the other churches revealed that further research would have been redundant.
• I chose the first five churches, in part, because they each hold one or more seminars per year for church leaders who want to know more about what they are doing in ministry, and why.

John Ed Mathison moved, in 1972, to be the pastor of **Frazer Memorial United Methodist Church** in Montgomery, Alabama. He inherited a staid traditional church averaging 150 in worship, with about 400 members. Since the city of Montgomery was scheduled to build a freeway through Frazer's choir loft, the church decided to relocate! Today, Frazer averages about 4,300 in attendance and has about 7,500 members. The church receives over 600 new members per year; more of them join as new Christians than as transfers from other United Methodist churches or from churches of other denominations. The church is best known for the involvement of its laity in ministries.

In that same year, 1972, Dale Galloway established **New Hope Community Church** in Portland, Oregon. Following a divorce, Galloway departed from his ecclesiastical roots in the Church of the Nazarene (though not from its Wesleyan theology) to establish New Hope as an independent church to reach broken people looking for new hope. The church pioneers in recovery ministries, and is best known for its extensive small groups. New Hope has 6,300 members, and receives about 500 new members per year—80 percent without a church from which to transfer. The church averages 3,000 in Sunday worship attendance and about 5,200 in weekly attendance in small groups.

In 1975, Bill Hybels and a group of young adults, all "graduates" of an innovative youth ministry, decided to plant a "church for the unchurched," for people who want to relate to God but cannot stomach traditional church. They first met in the Willow Creek theater in the northwest area of greater Chicago. Today, **Willow Creek Community Church** now has its own facility seating 4,600. Willow Creek is the most visible apostolic experiment in the U.S. today. The church is best known for its multiple weekend "Seeker Services"—featuring an orchestra, adult contemporary music, drama and the arts, and "relevant preaching," which attract more than 15,000 people each weekend.

In 1978, Walt Kallestad became pastor of the four-year-old, 200 member **Community Church of Joy** in the Glendale section of metropolitan Phoenix, Arizona. This first generation Lutheran (LCA) church had "plateaued" and become traditional in near-record time. After a painful transition, Kallestad persuaded the leaders to "dream big" and become a mainline denominational church devoted to reaching unchurched people. Kallestad, and associate pastor Tim Wright, offer five worship services per weekend—two traditional, one "country," and two "adult contemporary." They average over 2,600 in weekend attendance, and have 6,000 members (including children).

In 1980, Rick Warren planted the **Saddleback Valley Community Church** in Orange County, California, as a new breed, Southern Baptist, "purpose driven" church targeting unchurched pre-Christian people. The church worshiped for years in rented facilities—high school gyms, night clubs, and other places. Today, Saddleback meets on its own acreage in a high-tech tent that seats 2,300. Believing that "a Great Commitment to the Great Commandment and the Great Commission Will Grow a Great Church," this 4,600-member church averages over 9,000 in total attendance at four weekend "contemporary" services. In its short history, Saddleback has started twenty-four daughter congregations!

These five congregations represent five different denominational traditions and five distinct target populations and fields of mission. I reflected, for months, upon the data I gathered in observations, interviews, tapes, manuals, documents, and other sources from these congregations. A contemporary paradigm for the "Apostolic Congregation" was taking shape.

The ten major themes featured in this book represent all five churches as they are, or aspire to be. Briefer periods in four other churches, each pursuing its mission in four still-different contexts, confirmed the directions I perceived and added material for fleshing out the paradigm.

Tom Wolf became the pastor of **The Church on Brady** in 1969, and Carol Davis joined him as ministry director in 1973. This Southern Baptist church in East Los Angeles targets a range of ethnic minority populations—Mexicans, Latinos, Filipinos, Chinese, Vietnamese, Koreans, and even Middle Eastern peoples like Lebanese and Iranians—many in poverty. The Church on Brady may be the most "apostolic" of any congregation I studied. They baptize about 100 new Christians per year, they average planting one new congregation per year, and—from a membership base of only 700 full members, they currently have more members (twenty-one) serving as Southern Baptist missionaries across the earth than any other church in the Southern Baptist Convention! For years, the church has "lost" about 10 percent of its members per year to upward mobility and to their daughter congregations.

Dieter Zander founded **New Song Church** in 1986 as one of the first churches to target undiscipled "Baby Busters." Zander left in 1994, to become one of the teaching pastors at Willow Creek; he is succeeded at this innovative Conservative Baptist church by a team of leaders—Paul Kaak, Frank Selvaggop, Jeannie Letherer, and Duke Dreeger. The church's worship attendance, "Where the Flock Likes to Rock!" has not suffered in the leadership transition. Each Sunday, about 1,100 people attend one of New Song's three services at a middle school gymnasium in West Covina, California. New Song's leaders refer to their target population as "pre-Christians"—a positively nuanced term that I use in this book.

Mike Slaughter became the pastor of the 103-year-old 137-member **Ginghamsburg United Methodist Church** in 1979. The village of Ginghamsburg, Ohio has about 25 houses, which does not provide a likely setting for a growing church drawing widely from the north Dayton metropolitan area. Today the church is a "high expectation" church of 900 blue collar and white collar members who take discipleship and leadership seriously. The church averaged over 1,450 in attendance (spread over four services) in its most recent reporting year (and over 1,800 since moving into a new facility), and involves over 1,600 people per week in small groups. The church receives more new members as new Christians than by either transfer from other United Methodist churches or from churches of other denominations.

Steve Sjogren planted the **Vineyard Community Church** in Cincinnati in 1983. A decade later, the church holds six weekend "celebrations" to accommodate an average attendance of 2,000. In contrast to the reputation (deserved or undeserved) of the national Vineyard movement, the Cincinnati church targets unchurched pre-Christians rather than churched Christians! The Cincinnati Vineyard church features celebrative contemporary worship, small groups, recovery ministries, and "Servant Evangelism"—an innovative approach to penetrating a city. The church has averaged planting one daughter congregation per year, and aspires to "extend the contagious atmosphere of God's kingdom to every person in Cincinnati."

These nine churches are not perfect churches. Nor could they be. In reinventing the kind of local church that can reach lost people, they made it up as they went along! Nevertheless, traditional churches have much to learn from these pioneering churches. It remains to be seen whether the traditional churches of North America are sufficiently educable to join what may be the most promising Christian movement of our time.

This book continues the vision, and several themes, of my book *How to Reach Secular People* (Abingdon, 1992). Feedback from that book has convinced me that some church leaders do not "get" a full dose of Great Commission fever the first time they are exposed to it. A pastor telephoned one April, saying, "I sure like your book about reaching secular people. Our church is going to do that, next year!" I said, "Great! What are you doing this year?" "We are refurbishing the church parlor," he replied. I asked about their plans for year after next. He expressed hope for a new parsonage!

May I suggest that the cause of reaching the growing secular populations of North America is not a fad, or a new program, or something interesting to try for a year. The issue is no less than the identity and mission of the Christian congregation in every community of the American mission field. This book draws from the nine churches to portray the kind of church that perceives its identity, and affirms its mission, and effectively reaches many secular people.

I thank the leaders and people of these churches for what they are risking in behalf of all churches, and for their "second mile" cooperation that made this book possible. I thank Asbury Theological Seminary for the generous sabbatical policy that freed the time for the field research and writing, and for my colleagues in Asbury's School of World Mission and Evangelism—Ron Crandall, Eunice Irwin, Bob Tuttle, Darrell Whiteman, Matt Zahniser, Pat Richmond, and particularly Everett Hunt, for serving as dean this semester. I thank Carol Childress, Fred Smith, and Bob Buford of Leadership Network, in Tyler, Texas, for the financial support that made the field research possible.

Church for the Unchurched

CHAPTER ONE

✝

The Rebirth
of the Apostolic
Congregation

The Christian movement now faces its greatest opportunity in the Western world in the last three centuries. Christians have an even greater warrant for leaning into the future with confidence than when William Blake wrote these famous lines:

> I will not cease from Mental Fight,
> Nor shall my Sword sleep in my hand,
> Till we have built Jerusalem
> In England's green and pleasant Land.

True, most Christians in the U.S. and Europe do not know, or feel, such confidence in Christianity's future. They observe the numerical decline and the declining morale of the "mainline" churches of North America and the "state" churches of Europe. They observe many people trusting science, or medicine, or therapy, or education, or drugs, or some guru, or a "self-help" book, or seminar to meet their needs. They observe many people living as if there is no God, or at least no available God. They observe the invasion and spread of other religions from astrology to Zen, and the wide assumption that all religions are "the same" anyway. From such observations, Christianity's future looks more like retrenchment than any great contagious movement. Furthermore, when they see many denominational leaders more concerned with career advancement, or political correctness, or mere ecclesiastical affairs than with any mission to pre-Christian populations, they doubt that many of the denominations still have the vision to spread the faith.

Many of us are learning, however, to not expect denominational hierarchies and bureaucracies to lead the column of progress, that major paradigm shifts seldom occur in the establishment. Today, we find the real future of Christianity modeled in pioneering local churches. Moreover, we are learning to see our world through two lenses—"Secularity" and "Modernity"—which provide important keys to understanding our opportunity into the twenty-first century.

Secularity

Secularization, defined as the withdrawal of whole areas of life and thought from the Church's influence, has proceeded for 500 years and continues unchecked.[1] Indeed, secularity has accelerated in Europe since World War I, and in the U.S. since World War II. The Church enjoys less and less of the "home field advantage" it experienced in the "Christendom" period of Western history, when parish churches influenced virtually everyone in Western culture. Consequently, we observe an increasing number of "secular people"—who have navigated their whole lives beyond the serious influence of Christian churches. They have little or no Christian memory, background, or vocabulary. Many of them do not even know what we are talking about, and have little or no experience of "church."

The numbers of secular people are increasing more in this generation than they have in any other. This fact is partly reflected in George Gallup's occasional inquiries about religious training in people's background. In 1952, 6 percent of the American adults in Gallup's random sample reported they had no religious training. The figure in 1965 was 9 percent. In 1978 it was 17 percent.[2] While the graph fluctuates somewhat since 1978, its direction continues. We can now infer that, by the turn of the century, a third of all teenage and adult Americans will have no religious training in their background. When you add to that number the additional number of people who did once experience some "religious training" but they did not "get it," it did not "take," they cannot now recall it, and there is no sense in which it informs their life, we see that a majority of the people of the U.S. are functionally "secular."

Now, Christians can perceive secularity as a "threat," and they usually do, but it has a flip side. "Secular" only means that the people are not substantially influenced by Christianity, it does not mean they are "irreligious." Some are, but many secular people today are religious seekers, and virtually all people are seekers in some seasons of their lives. *Newsweek*'s theme issue on "The Search for the Sacred: America's Quest for Spiritual Meaning,"[3] reports that the religious quest has increased in recent years; that "now it's suddenly OK, even chic, to use the S words—soul, sacred, spiritual, sin."[4] The phenomenon is so widespread that "the seekers fit no particular profile,"[5] but people now are about as likely to look outside the Christian tradition as inside it—or to "pick and choose" from two or more religions. Years of living only in terms of what our five senses can apprehend of the material world has left people running on empty. Northwestern University's Roy Larson observes, "Living in a secular world is like living in an astrodome with a roof over the top."[6] Actually, the interest in Buddhism, or New Age, or Wicca, or medieval chant music, or angels, or environmental crusades is a sign of people's receptivity and an active seeking for Ultimate Reality. Jesus had to coach his first followers to "look around you, and see how the fields are ripe for harvesting" (John 4:35). As we will see, the churches today that perceive a receptive mission field, and engage it appropriately, are gathering great harvests.

Modernity

From the synergism of many historical events, the Western world became not only "secular," but also "modern"—from the impact of the eighteenth-century "Enlightenment," or the "Age of Reason."[7] Building on the earlier Renaissance, the Enlightenment swaggered into eighteenth-century Europe with colossal confidence in human reason. It produced the intellectual foundations for Western society for the next two centuries. The Enlightenment's teachings are more widely believed by more Western people than are the teachings of Christianity. In recent generations, its teachings have shaped most people's view of Reality more than has Christianity. What are those teachings? With some oversimplification of a complex movement, we can summarize eight of its teachings that have been especially important in shaping the worldview of Western people:

- The Enlightenment taught that human beings are basically rational. What separates humans from the beasts of the fields, forests, and jungles is not their creation in God's image but their capacity for reasonable thought.
- The Enlightenment taught that people are basically good. In a challenge to the Christian doctrine of Original Sin, the Enlightenment was confident of humanity's essential goodness. (Enlightenment leaders observed, of course, that people do not always behave in good or reasonable ways. They attributed this to the unjust or oppressive *environment* in which people live. Fix the system, and the rationality and goodness of people will surface—a half-truth that has been with us ever since.)
- Following Isaac Newton's discovery of gravity and the development of his orderly, predictable, machinelike, closed-system model of the universe, many Western people no longer expected (or they had trouble perceiving) miracles; the supernatural became optional, and God was uninvolved. This is called Deism.

21

- Enlightenment leaders taught that people could base morality on reasoning alone, without the aid of revelation or religion.
- Enlightenment leaders taught that we could build and manage cities and societies on reason alone, without reference to revealed values or church leadership.[8]
- The movement was confident that science and education would liberate humanity from its entrenched problems like poverty, crime, injustice, and war.
- The Enlightenment spread the confidence that all problems are solvable, and therefore progress is "inevitable."
- The Enlightenment's philosophy of "Natural Religion" taught that all religions are essentially the same. While Christianity, Hinduism, Buddhism, and Islam, for example, look very different from one another on the surface, the deeper you go in each, the more similar they become—because all religions are rooted in a common religious consciousness in the human heart.

Why the Western World Is Becoming *Postmodern*

However, Modernity has not fulfilled most of its promises, and so the Enlightenment worldview has become increasingly vulnerable. Many scholars in many fields have concluded that our world is becoming *postmodern*. The Enlightenment's teachings, which became the intellectual foundations of the modern Western world, have been questioned or abandoned—leaving Western humanity without a consensus worldview.

To be specific, most thinking people have abandoned the Enlightenment's Pollyanna view of human nature as simply good and rational; the Third Reich and the Holocaust exposed that myth. Scientists have discovered more mystery and surprise, especially at the most microscopic and macroscopic (outer space) levels, than the Newtonian clockwork paradigm accommodates, and more people now experience the supramundane and the supernatural more frequently than they did a generation ago.[9] No rationally based consensus morality has yet developed, in part because people now know that if the foundational values supporting an ethic are not revealed, then they are really a matter of enculturation, taste, or preference. (For example, what is the rational basis for believing in "the dignity of all human beings"?) No one has succeeded, in two centuries, in building a reasonable society. (Listen to the political speeches of almost any political campaign for verification!) Since the mushroom shaped cloud, people have seen that science could as easily destroy us as save us, and people are more realistic (if not disillusioned) about what education can achieve. While many people still believe that social progress is possible, we find no one still confident that it is inevitable. Society has not become the rational, humane, orderly world that the Enlightenment expected.

Scholars have studied the world's religions much more extensively since the Natural Religion philosophy was developed, and we now know that the Enlightenment view that all religions are essentially the same was wrong by about 180 degrees! We now know that religions are most alike at the surface. For example, each religion designates some people to serve a priestly function, each religion practices prayer or meditation, has rites of passage, holy places, and so on. The deeper you delve into the religions, the more different they appear! We now know that each major religious tradition is rooted in its own distinct core worldview, which is not "the same" as any other. So we now know that the first argument for the uniqueness of Christianity is the uniqueness of every major religious tradition!

Our New "Apostolic Age"

The shape of the Church's emerging opportunity thus looks like this:

- Christendom is largely dissolved, and the peoples of Europe and North America are increasingly secular.
- The Enlightenment, which provided the worldview for the secular West, is a spent force. Consequently, people are increasingly receptive to, and searching for, a satisfying worldview.
- We are, once again, in an Apostolic Age—much like the age that early Christianity engaged.

We can dramatize some of what this new apostolic age means, and what the policy of most churches means, in terms of the John 4:35 text (cited above) and another text in which Jesus used the "harvest" metaphor: "The harvest is plentiful, but the laborers are few; therefore ask the the Lord of the harvest to send out laborers into his harvest" (Luke 10:2).

Three things, today, are similar to the ancient world reflected in those texts.

First, due largely to the secularization of the West and the breakdown of the Enlightenment, the harvest is great once again. More and more people need, and seek for, a satisfying worldview and spiritual fulfillment.

Second, one reason that most of the churches fail to gather the harvests around them is that the Church still has trouble perceiving the harvest. From the Christendom legacy, most churches continue "doing church" as usual, as though most people in our communities are Christians, as though ministry is merely the nurture and care of existing Christians. Many church leaders are in denial regarding the growing number of secular pre-Christians in their community. In many cases, a church's leaders do not know many secular unchurched people, so they assume there aren't many.

Third, the Christian movement still has too few laborers to gather the harvest. In most traditional churches, we ask our people to share the good news and invite people to church involvement, and they don't do it. In many traditional churches, we admonish our people to share the faith and invite, and they don't do it. In some traditional churches, we provide good evangelism training; the people take the training, and like it, and believe evangelism is very important, but they still don't do it![10]

So, we can identify several factors today that are similar to the experience of the first-century church.

The New Shape of Today's Opportunity

We can also identify a couple of things today that are different—not only from the first century but also from the first half of this century. First, many laborers that we *do* have now come out of harvest fields empty-handed. Second, many traditional churches are no longer able to reach, receive, retain, and grow the receptive people in their ministry area.

These two facts have a common cause: the harvest has changed from, say, corn to wheat. We know how to harvest corn, but we have no experience harvesting wheat. So, going with what we know, we now enter wheat fields with our corn pickers. We fail to gather the harvest, and even destroy some of it while trying to gather it! To be specific, churches usually assume:

• What motivated us is what will motivate them.
• The approach that reached us is the approach that will reach them.
• They already know what we are talking about.
• They like the Church enough to be able to respond affirmatively.

So, our usual approach ignores the most important changes of the last half century. Somewhat like Europe before us, secularization has now advanced in North America to the point that, in Bonhoeffer's words, "The rusty swords of the old world are powerless to combat the evils of today and tomorrow."

To be more specific: Earlier in this century, the Sunday evening evangelistic service, the Sunday school, the revival, the camp meeting, the crusade, and one-to-one confrontational evangelism still fit American culture and still gathered harvests. Today, those traditional approaches to propagating the gospel are all spent forces, or nearly so. Some churches still rely on those approaches, with declining yields; other churches have abandoned those approaches, without replacing them.

Consequently, the vast majority of churches have not, within memory, reached and discipled any really secular persons! Many churches would be astonished if it ever happened, because many churches do not even intend to reach lost people outside their church's present circle of influence. Their main business is caring for their members.

This problem is compounded by another: while some approaches and methods of evangelism can be effective with secular populations, the target population in the U.S. is now so secular that, in most places, we can no longer graft a good evangelism program onto a traditional congregation and expect to reach and retain many secular people. Why? The Christians won't invite, and the unchurched people won't come (or won't return). (I contended in *How to Reach Secular People* that we cannot do effective evangelism without understanding, and adapting to, the social, historical, and cultural context of the target population. I am now contending that we cannot do effective evangelism apart from understanding the kind of church from which Christians would reach out to, and into which we can effectively receive, secular seekers.)

What Kind of Church Reaches Secular Unchurched Non-Christians?

In considering all of this, I have become obsessed with two questions: What kind of church can reach and disciple the growing number of secular people across our land? What can churches do to produce a witnessing, inviting people?

These questions have driven my field research for several years. I began asking Christians "Do you ever share the gospel with non-Christians, or invite them to church?" When Christians have said "no," I have learned to ask: "What would have to change in your church before you would feel free to do that?" Their answers enabled me to identify several pieces of the puzzle.[11]

Also, several years ago I began observing and interviewing in some churches that are effectively reaching secular people. Now, we all know that many churches are growing but they may not be reaching, or even targeting, secular people. We can observe this fact from a slightly different perspective through the categories provided in Lee Strobel's *Inside the Mind of Unchurched Harry and Mary*. Strobel distinguishes between four populations:[12]

25

1. Churched Christians
2. Churched Non-Christians
3. Unchurched Christians
4. Unchurched Non-Christians.

Churches differ in which of those populations they "target." Many growing churches effectively target unchurched Christians—people who believe but do not belong. Many "renewal" oriented churches show less "numerical growth" than "Kingdom growth" because they target churched non-Christians—helping nominal church members experience reconciliation with God and become genuine disciples. Some churches even target churched Christians from other churches! In this book, we are emphasizing churches with a sustained track record in reaching unchurched non-Christians.[13]

I discovered that the God who acts and reveals His possibilities in history began, in the 1970s, to raise up "Apostolic Congregations," appropriate to this new apostolic age that do target and reach unchurched pre-Christians. I have been especially studying the nine churches profiled in the Preface:[14]

1. Frazer Memorial United Methodist Church, Montgomery, Ala.
2. New Hope Community Church, Portland, Oreg.
3. Willow Creek Community Church, Barrington, Ill.
4. Community Church of Joy, Glendale, Ariz.
5. Saddleback Valley Community Church, Orange County, Calif.
6. The Church on Brady, East Los Angeles, Calif.
7. New Song Church, West Covina, Calif.
8. The Ginghamsburg United Methodist Church, Tipp City, Ohio
9. Vineyard Community Church, Cincinnati, Ohio

The "Apostolic" Church: One New Type of Church Among Many

Now, "apostolic" is a revered term of the Christian tradition, but it is not a trendy term for referring to churches today. Indeed, writers now refer to nontraditional churches (of various kinds) with a surprising range of terms, including:

Boomer churches
Buster churches
Contemporary churches
Full Service churches

High Expectation churches
Innovative churches
Megachurches
Metachurches
Mission Driven churches
New Tribe churches
Purpose Driven churches
Seeker churches
Seven-Day-A-Week churches
Turnaround churches
User-Friendly churches
Vibrant churches
Vital churches
Willow Creek type churches

I have resisted the temptation to feature any of those terms in referring to the churches who target secular unchurched pre-Christian people, for two reasons: First, none of these terms does justice to the best apostolic churches. In particular, these terms do not suggest either the deep roots from which these churches draw, nor the high ground they occupy. Second, what makes these churches different is not a single feature[15] like prayer, small groups, a guitar in the sanctuary, or seven-day-a-week scheduling, but a combination of multiple features that function synergistically.

So, some apostolic congregations target "Baby Boomers," but some do not. Some apostolic congregations are megachurches, but some are not—at least not yet! Some apostolic congregations were planted as new churches; some were established churches which turned around from previous decline. Apostolic congregations do reach out to "seekers," but they also engage pagans who are not (yet) seeking! Most apostolic congregations are contemporary, high expectation, innovative, purpose-driven, and user-friendly, but those terms do not unveil their essence. Willow Creek is the most visible apostolic congregation, but it was not the first, and many apostolic congregations vary from the Willow Creek model in some important ways. Most apostolic congregations feature "Seeker Services," but such services are the visible tip of a much larger iceberg. This project's purpose is to bring the rest of the iceberg to the surface, to demonstrate somewhat comprehensively the kind of church that releases its people for witness and invitation, and reaches and disciples unchurched pre-Christian people.

One more qualifier is necessary. I have discovered that no church, no matter how "apostolic" its orientation or its obsession, reaches unchurched pre-Christian people exclusively. The church that celebrates and communicates the gospel clearly and relevantly enough to engage unchurched pre-Christian people also engages many churched non-Christians. Furthermore, many unchurched Christians have been looking for this kind of church, and some churched Christians from other churches (who are weary of committee meetings and "playing church") feel constrained to switch to a church with a vision for reaching lost people. Several apostolic experiments that intended to reach only unchurched pre-Christians have found that they could not keep the others out! Besides, reaching unchurched pre-Christians alone would not underwrite the dreams of an apostolic congregation. The wallets of affluent pagans are typically the last part of their anatomy to be converted. The nonaffluent people with problems, addictions, and so on (that some apostolic congregations target) may never be able to fund the ministries that they and others need.

Nevertheless, apostolic churches target, and reach, unchurched pre-Christian people in significant numbers. For example, 38 percent of The Community Church of Joy's 6,000 members were totally unchurched, and 60 percent had not belonged to any church for at least five years before this church engaged them.

Defining the "Apostolic" Church

I call these churches "apostolic" because: (1) Like the root meaning of the term "apostle" and like the experience of the New Testament apostles[16] their leaders believe that they and the church are "called" and "sent" by God to reach an unchurched pre-Christian population. (2) Their theology and message center upon the gospel of early apostolic Christianity, rather than upon the narrower dogmatism, or the more vague "inclusive" theism, or the conventional moralism found in many traditional churches.[17] (3) Like the early apostles and their communities, these churches adapt to the language and the culture of their target population to communicate meaningfully the meaning of the ancient message. (4) They are remarkably similar to certain key features we find in early apostolic Christianity, in the Anabaptist, Pietist, and Methodist apostolic movements within Reformation Christianity, and in many growing Third World congregations today.[18] So, the "apostolic congregation" is not a new kind of church, but a fairly perennial form of the Church—especially in mission fields, like ours.[19] However, except for the prevailing features to be discussed, today's apostolic congregations are not all alike, any more than the first century apostolic congregations were all alike!

Top Ten Features of the "Apostolic Congregation": Part One

Apostolic congregations are different from traditional congregations in at least fifty ways. Consistent with the Italian philosopher Pareto, who once observed that there is (more or less) a "20/80" rule of thumb for all of life, I have identified ten distinctive features of apostolic congregations that account for about 80 percent of the difference. The first four will surprise no one.

1. Apostolic Congregations take a redundant approach to rooting believers and seekers in Scripture.

2. Apostolic Congregations are disciplined and earnest in Prayer, and they expect and experience God's action in response.

3. Apostolic Congregations understand, like, and have compassion for lost, unchurched, pre-Christian people.

4. Apostolic Congregations obey the Great Commission—more as warrant or privilege than mere duty. Indeed, their main business is to make faith possible for unreached people; evangelization is not merely one of many more or less equally important ministries of the church.

Most of us would assume that Christians (and churches) who (1) study the Scriptures, (2) pray expectantly, (3) love lost people, and (4) obey the Great Commission to the point of making outreach their priority business, are more likely to share their faith and invite people. These hunches are thus confirmed. We have no need to devote a chapter to each of those distinctives, though the four points warrant some elaboration in this chapter.

The first distinctive states that "Apostolic Congregations take a redundant approach to rooting believers and seekers in Scripture." I could illustrate this from any of the nine apostolic congregations, but one will suffice. The leaders of Ginghamsburg United Methodist Church believe that immersion in scriptural truth is the source of the church's identity, perspective, and apostolic vision. They believe that faith comes from hearing, and being shaped by, the Word of God; that Scripture is the primary source of the Christian's mind in an age of religious and philosophical anarchy; that open encounter with the Bible renews the Church; that with John Wesley and the other reformers, the Church is to live as a "People of One Book." Ginghamsburg's senior pastor, Mike Slaughter, observes that

> people are longing for a word from God. They are not interested in our personal opinions. They want more than the latest book review or political

29

commentary. Our people yearn for a message from God in an age of uncertainty and materialistic self-centeredness. In a time when the nuclear family is being redefined through divorce and single parenting, does God still speak with a voice of hope? In an age of global, political, and economic instability, growing racial tension, uncertain moral boundaries, and AIDS—is there a word from God? [20]

Because Scripture is so important, we find in apostolic churches an intentionally redundant approach to rooting people in the Book. (Effective churches often take a redundant approach to what they value as most important. They do not confine the impact of what is most important to what can be marketed or channeled through one approach or method.) Besides biblical preaching and regular Bible study in many strong Sunday school classes, such a church may feature the year-long Bethel, Navigator, Trinity, *and* Disciple Bible Studies, and many topical Bible studies, many thorough studies of books of the Bible, and many ongoing Bible study groups—all taught by many people, in many locations, at many different times, of a typical week.

The second distinctive states that "Apostolic Congregations are disciplined and earnest in Prayer, and they expect and experience God's action in response." Any of the nine congregations could serve as an exemplar, but the approach of The Community Church of Joy is notable. Associate Pastor Bjorn Pederson has led the church's prayer ministry for several years. Joy's prayer ministry involves 1,000 to 1,200 people per week.

The Community Church of Joy dispensed with the Wednesday evening prayer meeting; eight prayer meetings now congregate at the church at different times per week; each prayer meeting involves ten to twenty-five people and has a target group—like business people, or young women with children, or retired people, or a focus—like mission or healing. The church periodically schedules a "Prayer Retreat," and at other times a "College of Prayer"—typically featuring thirty or more courses led by as many instructors. One of a half-dozen trained prayer teams is available to people wanting to meet Christ, in a prayer chapel adjacent to the main sanctuary, following each weekend worship service. A team of ten lay people gives regular "Prayer Care" to people in hospitals, homes, and other places. Another team serves as "mentors" for people needing help in starting a life of prayer and devotion. Joy's prayer council organizes a remarkable "Prayer Partner" ministry; everyone in Joy's 6,000 membership has a prayer partner. The church organizes prayer groups, prayer chains, prayer walks, even occasional "prayer cruises"! A trained team of people responds to about fifty requests per week for intercessory prayer. Joy projects that one day the church will deploy its people in a 24-hour prayer telephone ministry.

Pederson and other leaders report that the prayer emphasis has brought great change to the church and its people. Many people have discovered God's truth, will, or guidance. Many have discovered their identity, self-worth, or spiritual fruits or gifts. Many people report answered prayers, answered intercessory prayers, spiritual empowerment, or victory over sickness or sin or the Evil One. People become more transparent with God and each other. The church experiences a unity and power it had not known before. Pederson and Joy's other prayer ministry leaders hold an annual conference for leaders from other churches wanting to develop prayer ministries.

The third distinctive states that "Apostolic Congregations understand, like, and have **compassion** for lost, unchurched, pre-Christian people." Every apostolic congregation stresses the importance of goodwill toward lost people, but none more memorably than Willow Creek Community Church. Willow Creek's cogent conviction that "Lost People Matter to God" is the driving force behind the church's mission to unchurched pre-Christian people.

Many traditional churches, by contrast, are essentially judgmental toward lost secular people. Many others seem to be motivated by the need to recruit more members to stop the decline, or pay the bills, or maintain the institutional church. Those are all understandable motives, but compassion drives churches to more authentic outreach and attracts many more seekers toward the faith and the faith community.

The fourth distinctive states that "Apostolic Congregations obey the Great Commission—more as warrant or privilege than mere duty. Indeed, their main business is to make faith possible for unreached people; evangelization is not merely one of many more or less equally important ministries of the church." Every apostolic congregation sees itself essentially as a "church for the unchurched," and their mission is to make faith and new life possible for people who do not yet believe or even know what we are talking about.

A traditional congregation's main business, by contrast, is to nurture and care for its members and their children. Most traditional congregations hope for growth—largely through biological and transfer growth. They have no plans or expectations for reaching pagans and would be astounded if it ever happened! Though they hope for membership growth, eight or nine out of ten traditional congregations are experiencing membership stagnation or decline.

However, the apostolic congregation's main business is outreach to pre-Christian people. That mission takes priority over ministry to the members. The outreach priority enables them to avoid what Roman Catholic missiologists call the "choke law" in which, after some growth, the church redirects the time and energy once devoted to outreach to care for the members, which "chokes" the ongoing mission to the remaining undiscipled population.

These features of apostolic churches, then, appear to shape their people in contagious ways. When Christians of apostolic congregations study scripture, connect to God, love sinners, and make the Great Commission their main business, they are more likely to reach out than are members of more traditional congregations.

Top Ten Features of the "Apostolic Congregation": Part Two

Besides those four features—Scripture, Prayer, Love, Obedience—that are most obvious, this project has identified six more features of apostolic congregations that are not as obvious:

5. Apostolic congregations have a motivationally sufficient vision for what people, as disciples, can become.

6. Apostolic congregations adapt to the language, music, and style of the target population's culture.

7. Apostolic congregations labor to involve everyone, believers and seekers, in small groups.

8. Apostolic congregations prioritize the involvement of all Christians in lay ministries for which they are gifted.

9. The members of Apostolic Congregations receive regular pastoral care. They are in regular spiritual conversation with someone who is gifted for shepherding ministry.

10. Apostolic Congregations engage in many ministries to unchurched non-Christian people.

In the chapters that follow, chapter 2 fleshes out the apostolic vision of what people can become; chapter 3 makes the case for the "culturally indigenous" congregation; chapter 4 is devoted to the role of small groups in apostolic congregational life and strategy; chapter 5 shows how lay ministry is the key to a lay apostolic movement. I have not written distinct chapters for the ninth and tenth points. I include the point about pastoral care within the chapter on lay ministry. I show, in the two chapters on small groups and lay ministries, how apostolic congregations typically minister to secular unchurched people. The insights regarding the apostolic "shape" of these churches are not all new. Indeed, *The Emerging Church*, by Bruce

Larson and Ralph Osborne, anticipated several of these same themes a quarter century ago.[21]

I have discovered that the kind of church from which outreach would emerge does matter, that Christians in apostolic congregations are, say, 10 to 15 times more likely to engage in witnessing and inviting than Christians in traditional congregations. A review of these six features quickly suggests why:

1. Christians are more likely to witness and invite if they have a vision of what people can become that goes deeper than accepting our beliefs, obeying our rules, or conforming to our style.

2. The members of a culturally relevant church are much more likely to invite their friends to a worship service they would like their friends to experience than to a service they would dread for their friends to experience!

3. Christians who regularly discuss the gospel, and share what God is doing in their life, in a small group are much more likely to share these matters in their other relationships.

4. People who are involved in a lay ministry, for which they are gifted and in which they experience God working, are much more likely to engage in the ministry of evangelism.

5. People who are in regular spiritual conversation with a pastor or spiritual mentor are much more likely to engage in spiritual conversations with people who are not yet Christians.

6. Churches with ministries to the needs of unchurched pre-Christians thereby build more bridges to the people, have greater credibility with them, find them to be much more receptive, and experience many more "natural" opportunities for faith sharing.

Members of apostolic churches typically experience a profound paradox: Church members, say, who have caught the apostolic vision for people, who experience celebrative indigenous worship, who are involved in pastoral conversation, and in a small group, and in a gift based ministry, and are involved in ministry with pre-Christian people (and are studying scripture, praying, and so on) are themselves far more blessed and "ministered unto" than if they had their own hired chaplain in a small traditional church. (Furthermore, seekers are far more interested in joining such a church than a traditional church.)

This, however, is the supreme point of this project. The church with apostolic features typically produces much more of an apostolic laity.[22] For example, a recent survey of the Community Church of Joy's adult membership revealed that 81 percent of the members had invited at least one person during the past year. Eighteen percent had invited seven or more persons! With the exception of new churches, I seldom find traditional congregations activating much more than a tenth of that number of members for outreach. Furthermore, there are no reasons to believe that The Community Church of Joy has reached the ceiling of what is possible in producing a contagious laity.

✝

What People Can Become

I was preaching for the two morning services at a church in the Midwest. At the coffee fellowship period between the two services, I visited with a couple who were new Christians. They had visited the church to find "some glue" for their marriage; they found much more. I asked them, "How is it going in your new life as Christians?"

The husband responded with an unusual analogy. "Sometimes, we feel like we have joined a bowling team. We come every Sunday, and Wednesday nights when we can. We come dressed to bowl, each of us carrying a bowling ball. [He held up his Bible.] We step up to the line to bowl, but we can't see the pins! Some church leaders have hung a sheet in front of the ten pins, so we can't see the pins. After we bowl, they tell us how many pins we hit."

His wife jumped in with "No Dear, they tell us how many pins we missed!"

Then they barraged me with questions. "Shouldn't we be allowed to see the pins? How can we hit the pins if we can't see them? Don't we have a right to see the pins?" They followed with one very perceptive question: "We know that being a real Christian is not just one thing; it has got to be several, maybe even a dozen—but what are they?"

What Is the Target?

I have often reflected upon their analogy, and their question. What are the "pins" for which God is aiming the lives of Christians? Coincidentally, the word most often used in the New Testament that we translate as "sin"—*hamartia*—was borrowed from archery, and meant to miss the target! So, what is the target? The question is serious for a church's mission because a "motivationally sufficient vision" of what people, by grace, can become is a key factor in whether or not many people of a church reach out.

What are our hopes for people? If God's dreams for a person were realized, how would that person be different? How would that person now live? What difference does becoming a Christian make? What difference should it make?

I have found, with some digging, two contrasting kinds of answers to this question. One kind of answer is typical of traditional congregations, whose people do not generally engage in outreach. The other kind of answer is typical of apostolic congregations, whose people are much more likely to share their faith and invite people.

The Midwestern couple assumed that the leaders in their church knew the goals of a Christian's life but weren't telling! However, the matter is not much more clear to traditional church leaders than it is to new Christians and seekers. Most church leaders assume certain answers to this question, but in traditional churches the answers are seldom spoken. Leaders of apostolic congregations are more likely to have reflected upon this matter, but part of their answer is still assumed.

In probing to identify a church's assumed goals for people, I have learned to observe various cues and clues. For example, sometimes a church's goals for people are suggested in what they measure, and report—like church attendance or baptisms. Sometimes the goals are revealed in the standards for membership, or the standards for leaders. Sometimes the goals are indicated in whom the core members are and are not friendly with, or about whom and what people gossip (or brag), or the values inferred from whom they nominate as the heroes and heroines of their church's history, and from the stories they tell about them. Sometimes it is useful to ask, "How do you tell who is a real Christian?" This question reveals, at least, the indicators in their minds.

The Goals for People in Traditional Churches

Over the years, from this admittedly unscientific detective work, I have been able to observe, infer, and verify at least ten widely used goals that traditional churches often have in mind for people. I propose to state these assumptions, and unpack them, and show at least one historical precedent for each (to demonstrate they are long with us), and then ask whether they are adequate and motivating objectives for Christian evangelism.

1. One group of traditional churches simply wants people to **"be religious,"** and they will accept almost any kind of religious orientation from anyone who will still claim to be religious. This stance is characteristic of some liberal churches, and is partly a reaction against the Enlightenment.

The Enlightenment's view of the cosmos, from Isaac Newton, scripts people to think of the entire universe as a self-contained machine that does not need a God to manage it. Consequently, many modern people doubt the existence of anything "beyond" the material universe. These churches, however, still believe in (and perhaps experience) the Numinous, or the Transcendent, or the Supernatural.

These churches are also partly co-opted by the Enlightenment. The philosophy of "Natural Religion" that developed during the Enlightenment taught that all religions, at their core, are essentially the same—because, they proposed, all religions are rooted in a common religious consciousness that all people share. So, some forms of liberal Christianity—influenced by the Natural Religion idea and reacting against the Enlightenment's antisupernaturalism, find themselves celebrating (and wanting to include) anybody who still believes in anything beyond the empirical world! "If you believe in a God (or "Higher Power") of any kind, you're one of us."

2. A second group of traditional churches is not as indifferent to the content of belief; indeed, they want people to **"believe like us."** Many of these churches are theologically conservative, but not all. Some churches expect certain beliefs characteristic of liberation theology, or black theology, or feminist theology, or "politically correct" ideology. (In such a church, not long ago, I learned that I am not "bald" after all; I am "follicly challenged!") The conservative churches who stress beliefs are combating the Enlightenment ideology that introduced "pluralism," and theological anarchy, in many minds and societies. Such a church's challenge to secularity emphasizes beliefs in revealed doctrines; the test of faith becomes a person's intellectual assent to theological truth claims. One precedent for this emphasis is ancient Gnosticism—which taught that the redeemer figure had descended through the eons down to earth to bring human beings the saving information; to hear and believe that information was to be saved. Some branches of the Church have, to some degree, emphasized faith as assent in much of Christianity's history.

3. Some churches want people to **"behave like us."** These churches have clear moral rules—behavioral prescriptions and prohibitions, to which "faithful" people conform. We find a precedent in the ancient Pharisees— with whom Jesus contended, who had over 100 rules for what you could and could not do on the Sabbath and, I am told, over 1,000 rules altogether.

The Pharisees are still with us, in Christian clothing! In England, a church woman observed some divinity school students going into a movie theater on Sunday. She complained to their pastor. The pastor attempted to help her "open up," explaining that Jesus allowed his disciples to pick grain on the Sabbath. She replied, "Yes, and two wrongs don't make a right!"

On a more serious note, there are many specific contexts—like the rough frontier towns of the nineteenth century and the crime, drugs, and AIDS threatened cities of the twentieth century, that influence churches to emphasize moral norms as the test of faithfulness. Nevertheless, Christianity's public image is excessively equated with mere moralism, so traditional churches need to rediscover the issues that transcend mere morality. As Martin Luther commented, "Morality is the concern of lawyers, judges, and hangmen. My concern is your God relation."

4. Some traditional churches project for people **"an experience like ours."** The goal is a normative type of religious experience. The particular type of experience will vary from one tradition to another. For some churches the normative experience is emotional—as in a repentance experience, accompanied by tears, at a camp meeting or revival service. For some "high" churches the experience is more aesthetic—like the awe one experiences in hearing Bach on a great pipe organ or in viewing Michelangelo's Sistine Chapel. For still other churches the normative experience is ecstatic—like speaking in tongues, in a Charismatic or Pentecostal service. One ancient precedent for an experiential approach is the ancient Mystery Religions—in which it was believed that salvation is transmitted through religious experiences.

5. Some traditional churches want other people to **"become like us"** culturally. For these churches, the sign of conversion or religious authenticity is the reinculturation of the new (or prospective) member. In this model, we know they are "one of us" when they talk like us, dress like us, see the world like us, and share our tastes—from food to sports to "our kind of music."

The existence of this model is more clear to non-Christians than to Christians. Most non-Christians are very aware that, in most churches, "becoming like church people" is a requirement for becoming a Christian, but the requirement functions at a more subconscious level within church people. "They" experience "us" to require more conformity than we are conscious of. Nevertheless, the leaders of any church can identify, when asked, many names of visitors, inactive members, and dropouts who "just didn't fit in."

We find an ancient precedent for this approach in the "Judaizers"—the first century Christians, led by James and the Jerusalem church, who expected Gentiles to become circumcised, give up pork, obey sabbath laws, and adopt many other Jewish customs as a precondition to becoming followers of Jesus.

6. Some traditional churches believe that Christianity's objective is for people to **"be good citizens."** Loren Mead, in *The Once and Future Church*, reminds us that in ancient and medieval Christendom "the ministry of the

layperson was identical with being a good, law-abiding, tax-paying, patriotic citizen."[1] I am told that, even in the late Roman Empire, Caesar's devotees sported bumper stickers on their chariots saying "The Roman Empire, Love It Or Leave It!"

In the U.S., Christianity and patriotic citizenship have often been closely linked. In the nineteenth century, this branch of American Christianity believed that God had a "Manifest Destiny" for the U.S., that provided the spiritual vision for "winning the West." In the late twentieth century, "American Civil Religion" assumes that the values of "the American Way of Life" are synonymous with the values of the kingdom of God.

7. Some traditional churches expect members to **"share our politics."** Historically, the European State Churches have generally supported conservative politics, and the Free Churches have often supported liberal politics. Fairly early in this century, many American mainline Protestant churches aligned themselves with the Democratic Party. More recently, many conservative churches have departed from their earlier neutrality and aligned themselves with the Republican Party.

Indeed, many denominations spotlight one or two moral causes that need the support of law to be implemented. For instance, many Black churches (and some Anglo churches) have focused on civil rights. Several denominations, such as Quakers, Brethren, and Mennonites, have rallied their people around peace. Some churches enlist their members against pornography, and others against the exploitation of nature. Around the abortion issue today, some churches are so "pro-life" and others are so "pro-choice" that neither church would be likely to have any members publicly on the other side.

8. Some churches (and denominations) expect people to **"support the institutional church."** This objective, I think, is essentially a modern blemish on the Body of Christ, but I suppose we can find precedents—as a medieval pope's sale of indulgences to pay for St. Peter's Cathedral. In this model, the "good Christians" let us put their names on the church rolls; they attend church regularly, and they attend meetings, serve on committees, carry out various maintenance tasks, and give generously to the church's budget—without annoying questions about where their money goes. The "good Christians" are the people the institutional church can count on.

9. Some traditional churches have the goal of **"preparing people for heaven."** For them, Christianity is essentially an "eternal life insurance policy," or a "fire escape!" Life in this world afflicts people with "achy breaky hearts," but accepting Christ assures us of a better life in the next world.

This view of the essence of Christianity is remarkably widespread. Going to heaven, and preparing for the journey, is the dominant theme of both "gospel music" and country and western religious music. This image of the Christian religion was in the mind of Karl Marx when he branded it "the opium of the people." Virtually all discussion, by Christians, about whether people of other religions "can be saved" assumes that going to heaven is Christianity's central point. Furthermore, some of the training programs in evangelism begin by asking people whether they are going to heaven.

It is quite true that New Testament Christianity proclaimed that "Christ is raised," so therefore "nothing, including death, will ever separate us from the love of God," and that Christ has gone "to prepare a place for us." Nevertheless, early Christianity never saw "going to heaven" as the only point, or even the main point, behind the incarnation, teaching, crucifixion, and resurrection of Christ and the gift of the Spirit to God's people. The New Testament proclaims multiple outcomes for God's action—including forgiveness, justification, reconciliation, new birth, sanctification, and life within the reign of God. The ancient Mystery Religions and the Gnostic religions treated the afterlife as the only point, but Apostolic Christianity did not.

I have placed this goal for people near the end of traditional church goals for people, because many apostolic congregations also feature it. However, even in apostolic congregations, this does not appear to be a "motivationally sufficient" goal for propelling God's people into outreach. Virtually no one in apostolic congregations who reaches out has heaven as their only goal for people, and few have it as their primary goal. They are (even) more concerned about people who are living without Christ than about people who are dying without him.

10. Some churches have explicit **"sacramental"** goals for people. This approach comes in two forms. "High Church" leaders hope to see people baptized as infants and later confirmed into the Church. They want people to receive holy communion and, in some churches, offer confessions and receive last rites. They believe that the grace of our Lord Jesus Christ is dispensed to people, by his Body the Church, through the sacraments that were "dominically instituted" by Christ himself.

The "Low Church" version of sacramental goals for people accents the "devotional life." A Christian reads the Bible and prays daily, a Christian family has prayer together at meals and at bedtime. An industry of books and devotional guides has emerged around this paradigm. The "best churches" have the largest subscriptions to *The Upper Room* bimonthly devotional guide. We find precedents for the High Church emphasis fairly early in Christianity, and today in Roman Catholic, Lutheran, and Anglican churches, and in the European State Churches. Important precedents to the devotional approach include Monastic Catholicism and early Protestant Pietism.

Both the high church and low church sacramental models illustrate the confusion, often evolved over time, that mistakes means for ends. The Sacraments and other sacramental practices were originally means of grace. They were conduits for knowing God and his will, they were channels for gaining the spiritual power to live out God's will. When the means got substituted for the ends, a Christian became someone who attends Mass or reads the Bible. Apostolic churches have a sacramental emphasis also, high or low, but they are more clear than traditional churches about means and ends.

An Assessment of the Traditional Church's Goals for People

I have delineated ten objectives for people that I often observe in traditional churches—conservative, liberal, or both. One of these goals does not often live by itself in the minds of a church's leaders; usually two, or three, or four of these objectives will occupy the same room. For instance, I recently consulted in a church that expected people to be good Americans who become like us, behave like us, and support the church as an institution, but the other six traditional goals for people were not prominent in this church.

You may be asking what is "wrong" with these objectives for people that often operate in traditional churches. There is nothing "wrong" with any of them and much to commend most of them. Perhaps a personal confession will clarify my point: I am an orthodox theologian who believes that orthodoxy is the vertebrae of the Body of Christ, but I know that the devil believes, and that faith goes deeper than beliefs. I know that moral norms are important ingredients in any glue that holds a life, a family, a community, or a society together. I want people to be able to face death with assured hope rather than paralyzing fear. I know that true faith is usually an experienced faith. I know the sacraments, scripture, and prayer to be means of real grace. I affirm, and exercise, my American citizenship. I believe that, in the words of Hugh Price Hughes, "What is morally wrong cannot be politically right!" On most days, I am even sure that the church as an institution is worth supporting. I sympathize with every religion's struggle to maintain a sense of the supernatural in a secular technological world. I will even admit that I am often more comfortable with people who are like me culturally, though my comfort level is not a sufficient reason for expecting other people to change!

Furthermore, I would not pretend that these goals are irrelevant to Christianity. Some of these goals may, indeed, precede faith. For example, one man believed that Jesus is God's revelation before he ever met him, and his wife had several experiences of answered prayer before she finally committed to Christ and his will for her life. Some of these objectives may accompany faith, as in the case of a new believer who said he was already "more relaxed about death"! Some of these objectives typically follow new faith—like new moral behaviors.

I have not unpacked these traditional objectives because they are bad, nor because they are irrelevant, but because they do not sufficiently reflect essential Christianity, and they are not sufficient motivators to drive congregations to fulfill their mission; therefore, they are not adequate to serve as a congregation's driving objectives for people. Indicators yes; objectives no. It would be possible to realize most of these goals within one's life and still not be a New Testament Christian. These goals are not essentially what we are called to aim at, because they are not essentially why Christ came, lived, died, was raised, and gave his Spirit to the Church.

Perhaps we can see the need for rethinking this matter from a case in point. In the mid-1980s Tatiana Goricheva, a young philosophy student at Leningrad University, lost her confidence in dialectical materialism. She then became an existentialist, but when that philosophy did not meet the deepest needs of her soul, she turned to Yoga. She tells what happened next:

> In a yoga book a Christian prayer, the "Our Father," was suggested as an exercise. . . . I began to say it as a mantra, automatically and without expression. I said it about six times, and then suddenly I was turned inside out. I understood . . . that he exists. [God], the living, personal God, who loves me and all creatures, who has created the world, who became a human being out of love, the crucified and risen God.[2]

Imagine that Tatiana has become a graduate student in the U.S., that she has joined your church, and she is open to everything Christianity has to offer. Are you really content, say, to have her swear by a creed, give up her occasional vodka, take on our customs, bring her offering envelope every Sunday, serve on a committee, and prepare for heaven? Is there any more to it than that? Is that the faith that can change the world? What is our game plan for Tatiana?

The Goals for People in Apostolic Congregations

I observe many of the new apostolic congregations beginning to model an alternative game plan for people. While they would sympathize with most of the traditional church's goals for people, and they would take a dim view of the Christian seriousness of any professing Christian who, say, denied the deity of Christ, lived immorally, and espoused Sino-Communism, their emphasis for people points toward a distinct, and contrasting, set of goals. Most of the apostolic congregations I studied have given the "goals for people" issue some conscious attention, but their model-building is not yet finished.

For example, Willow Creek Community Church's strategy for helping people "to become fully devoted followers of Jesus Christ" focuses on these four goals for Christians:

- Regular worship in the believers' (New Community) service
- Involvement in a small group
- Involvement in a ministry for which the Christian is gifted
- Friendship building and witness to unchurched pre-Christian people

Again, the leaders of New Song Church, fleshing out a similar mission statement, have developed an impressive set of articles:

Five Vital Signs of Growth
(or, "How we know we are fulfilling the vision God has called us to.")

The saints can say:

I am growing in my intimacy with God and faithfulness to His word.

This vital sign is demonstrated in my life by spending time with God through prayer, worship, listening to Him, reading the Bible and actively living out His principles in my life.

I am growing in real relationships with others in a small group.

This vital sign is demonstrated in my life by gathering with others to actively use my spiritual gifts, to build them up in Christ, and to be involved in disciple making.

I am growing in my service to God and others.

This vital sign is demonstrated by discovering my unique God-given gifts, passions, and personality, selflessly and effectively to serve my family, my church, and my community so that God's kingdom and work can be furthered.

I am growing in reaching my pre-Christian relationships for Christ.

This vital sign is demonstrated by my growing compassion and ability to build friendships with pre-Christians that will lead to an opportunity to introduce them to Jesus.

I am growing in my sensitivity toward the training of leaders and planting of groups and churches.

This vital sign is demonstrated by my enthusiasm to support God's heart to develop individuals and teams to strategically extend God's kingdom nearby and far away.

Those five articles are impressive, but a couple of them really involve multiple goals, a couple of them are more signs of Christian seriousness than goals, and one relates specifically to an emphasis of that church that would not necessarily be a primary goal for all Christians. So we need more reflection upon our goals for people within today's apostolic movement.

We are not mounting a case for a "Christian cloning" program that would force everyone into the same mold. We are created with different personalities, talents, and strengths, and the Holy Spirit gives us different spiritual gifts for ministry. As no two bowlers are the same, so we should not expect all Christians to be the same. Yet, like bowlers, we are all involved in the same game, so some of the pins we are all aiming for should be the same. But what are they? This makes for an interesting forced-choice exercise. If you had to identify the ten pins (no more and no less) for which God targets the lives of all Christians, what would they be?

Christian leaders occasionally address this question in memorable ways. John Calvin's echo in the Westminster Confession affirms that "the chief end of man is to glorify God and enjoy Him forever." Willow Creek wants "irreligious people to become fully devoted followers of Jesus Christ." My Midwestern couple wants to "glorify God" and become "fully devoted followers of Jesus Christ" but, like many people, they want to know more specifically what that means.

One day, I realized that this was essentially the question that John Wesley was addressing in his remarkable eighteenth-century essay "The Character of a Methodist." Standing on Mr. Wesley's shoulders, I have developed a model that reproduces several of his "pins," but which also interfaces afresh with the Scriptures, and with the wider Reformation tradition, and also with my observations of apostolic congregations and my interviews with first generation converts out of secularity. In the model I now commend, each of the ten pins is named, and each row of pins is also named. The one pin in the first row deals with what most modern secular people need to **Discover** before they can effectively begin the Christian pilgrimage. The second row, with two pins, features what God wants all people to **Experience**. The third row, with three pins, identifies the essential features of the **New Life** in Christ. The fourth row, with four pins, focuses on the **New Lifestyle** to which Christ calls us.

The Discovery

Focusing on the one pin in the first row, the New Possibility that God offered in Jesus Christ commonly begins for people with the profound discovery, simply stated in Willow Creek's credo, that we "matter to God." It often begins with this discovery, because most secular people do not yet know they matter to God. They may never have even guessed it because, while they believe in a God (the vast majority of secular people are not atheists), they are "Deists."

Deists, today, come in two types.

We find the first type of Deist in the majority of secular people who, throughout their lives, have harbored the mental model of God reflected in the "Watchmaker" analogy of the philosopher John Locke. They believe, or assume, that a Transcendent Mind created the universe and got everything started, but then removed himself, is no longer involved, and no longer cares. I interviewed two men, both confessing Deists. One commented, "If I saw a baseball, with the two equally shaped pieces of leather stitched so precisely, I would know that it did not come together like that by accident; it has a designer and a maker. If I saw a baseball the size of a house, I would conclude the same. So, when I see a ball the size of the world, and infinitely more complex than a baseball, I reason that it too must have a designer and maker. There's got to be a Big Mind behind the Big Bang." Then his colleague chipped in: "But Bob and I are only two of five billion people on this planet. This world is but one of nine planets in our solar system, our sun is but one of a hundred million stars in our galaxy, and our galaxy is but one of a hundred million galaxies in the known universe. Granting what we know about the vastness of space, it is a stretch to believe that we matter to God." Their "god" is the Absentee Landlord of the cosmos.

We find the second type of Deist in the minority of secular people who once believed in a more personal God than Deism knows, but they have experienced or observed too much pain, suffering, tragedy, violence, and injustice. As they observe "Truth forever on the scaffold, Wrong forever on the throne," their earlier Pollyanna assumptions about God and life are undermined by life experiences; they conclude that "God must not be involved, after all," and they move into Deism, occasionally into Atheism.

We find the most potent material for helping the first group, the Lifetime Deists, in the actual message of Jesus. In Luke 15, Jesus tells the three parables of the lost sheep, the lost coin, and the lost son. Those parables have five ideas in common: (1) Something of great value is lost. (2) In response to this loss, there is an all-out search, or an anguished vigil. (3) When the lost is found, there is a great celebration. (4) God searches like the shepherd, the woman, and the father. (5) He does this because, like the sheep, the coin, and the son, we matter supremely to the Searcher. In the Sermon on the Mount, Jesus declares that God clothes the lilies of the fields, and we matter to God even more. A sparrow cannot fall to the earth without the Father's concern, and we matter to him even more. He knows us so well, Jesus taught, that even the hairs on our heads are numbered. From time to time, the Christian tradition has retrieved and spotlighted this profoundly simple teaching. Augustine declared that "God loves each one of us as if there was only one of us to love." Søren Kierkegaard counseled people to "read the Bible as though it were a letter from God with your personal address on it."

The second group, the Disillusioned Deists, are often helped by this message from Jesus that we "matter to God." But they are more deeply reached by the message about Jesus—especially the gospel of the Incarnation, that God "emptied himself, taking the form of a slave, being born in human likeness," that "the Word became flesh and lived among us." The doctrine of the Incarnation affirms that the God to whom we matter does not care for us from a safe distance—like a general at headquarters is concerned for his troops under siege. He is "Emmanuel"—"God is with us" —who paces the floor with us, suffers with us, and shares in the struggles of our lives. As James Russell Lowell affirmed, in "The Present Crisis":

> Careless seems the great Avenger; history's
>   pages but record
> One death-grapple in the darkness 'twixt
>   old systems and the Word;
> Truth forever on the scaffold, Wrong forever
>   on the throne,—
> Yet that scaffold sways the future, and, behind
>   the dim unknown,
> Standeth God within the shadow, keeping
>   watch above his own.[3]

The message that we matter this much to God is the leading edge of Christianity's gospel today. It is not the whole gospel, but it is the part that people typically discover first, and without this first discovery, they seldom discover the rest. They may discover this claim from reading Jesus' teaching, or through the sharing of some Christian friend or group. Sometimes they conduct an "experiment of faith," and try living their life as though they matter to a God who is with them, and they find the experiment self-authenticating. Often their experiment of faith includes prayer, and their experiences of answered prayer validate Jesus' good news that we matter to God.

The New Relationships

The second row has two pins, each featuring a normative experience in becoming a Christian. These two experiences can take place in a person's life in either order. I present them in the "logical" order, even though they usually occur in the opposite order.

One pin features a person's experience of **a new relationship with God.** This is the supreme promise of the Bible—that we shall know God, that we shall know the forgiveness, acceptance, and love of God, that we shall have his new covenant written upon our hearts, that we shall be born anew from above and shall know the power of God and the life of eternity within us (and among us). This faith relationship with God comes to us by sheer grace; we can never deserve it or earn it because we are sinners. As Stephen Neill explained, "All men are in a state of alienation from God; each man is the center of his own world, and claims the right to determine his own existence. This is rebellion and the way of death."[4] But, in the death of Jesus on a cross, "God showed his love for us"—a greater love than even our love of ourselves—and this greater love pulls us out of ourselves and invites us to respond to God in faith. Martin Luther once defined this faith as "a living daring confidence in the grace of God, so sure and certain that a man would stake his life on it a thousand times." This "leap of faith" (Kierkegaard) is the response to God's grace that reconciles us to God, and brings us out of death into life, and into a new relationship with God. So, "By grace [we] have been saved through faith, and this is not [our] own doing; it is the grace of God."

To be sure, in this new relationship with God, we still "see in a mirror, dimly, but then we will see face to face." The relationship with God we now experience is what Paul called a down payment, or a foretaste, or the first fruits of the fuller relationship with God that we will know one day. In the hymn "I Am Thine, O Lord," Fanny Crosby echoes this reality in the affirmation,

> There are depths of love that I cannot know till I cross the narrow sea;
> There are heights of joy that I may not reach till I rest in peace with thee.

God gives us this first installment of a relationship with him in this fallen world that is not yet the promised City of God. This first installment is enough. It provides moments in which we know God, and more moments in which we know that we are known, and this experience shapes us to live as God's People in the world.

If the first experiential pin features the Christian's new relationship with God, the other pin features **a new relationship with the People of God,** the Church. In Wesley's words, "Christianity is not a solitary religion," but a social religion; it is not an individual game like golf or weight lifting, but a team game like football or basketball. The Church is the Messianic Community, the Body of Christ, the New Israel. Becoming a Christian necessarily involves joining this People, for Jesus promised to be present where "two or three are gathered" in his name. Many people experience the Church, in some form, before they experience the faith relationship with God; that is natural, because the faith is "more caught than taught," and one's experiences in the Church should be more stacked on the side of faith than one's experiences in a fallen world. Furthermore, as many people discover faith inside the Church, so the faith of all Christians is nurtured inside the Church—by involvement in "the apostles' teachings, the fellowship, the breaking of bread, and the prayers." Moreover, the faith that is discovered and nourished in the Church is also retained in the Church; my interviews with people who once believed (but now believe no longer) reveal that people who drop out of the church are vulnerable, in time, to the breakdown and loss of faith—because Christianity is a communal faith.

The new apostolic churches are rediscovering that a fulfilling experience in the Church necessarily requires involvement in two structures. Wesley called his version of these two structures the society and the class meeting; most people experience these two structures as the worshiping congregation and the small group. Many people are involved in the congregation, and are thus involved in its proclamational, sacramental, and liturgical life, but not in the cell; they therefore never experience half of what "church" has to offer. Only in the church's redemptive cells do we really know each other, and support each other, and pull for each other, and draw strength from each other, and weep with each other, and rejoice with each other, and hold each other accountable, and identify each others gifts, and experience what it means to be "members of one another." That is why Bruce Larson claims that "it is just as important that you be involved in a small group as it is to believe that Jesus Christ died for your sins." There are some things that God can only do for us through the redemptive cell.

The New Life

The third row, with three pins, identifies what is basic in the new life that we now live—from our faith in Christ and involvement in his Church.

One feature of our new life is **doing the will of God.** As new Christians, we discover that we are no longer our own, but his, for we have been bought with a price. Now that we are reconciled to God, Christ calls us to "strive first for the kingdom of God and his righteousness." Paul explained that Christ "died for all, so that those who live might live no longer for themselves, but for him who died and was raised." So, as Wesley explained, "The one design of the Christian's life" is to do God's will, not his or her own will; the Christian's one intention now is to please God. Wesley explains that doing God's will means, first, obedience to God's commandments, "from the least to the greatest." Wesley explains that doing God's will also involves devoting our talents to God's purposes. So, the faith in which we live is an "obedient faith" (Emil Brunner).

New Christians often report that they are now living, or are at least striving to live, by God's will for their lives. They especially report a great difference in their motivational drive: before discovering God's grace, they tried to obey God's Law or live a good life because they aspired to earn God's acceptance or justify their lives; but now that they have experienced God's free acceptance, and know that God already justifies their lives, they now obey God out of gratitude. Furthermore, new Christians are often excited in the discovery that God can, and wants to, use their talents for his Purposes. New Christians report greater meaning in their lives, purpose for their lives, and satisfaction in their souls knowing that they are in tune with, and sometimes in line with, God's purposes for their lives and the world.

A second feature of the Christian's new life is a **love for people,** and for God's other creatures. Jesus taught us that the second great commandment, after loving God, is to "love your neighbor as yourself." This love (*agape* in New Testament Greek) is not so much a feeling of the heart as a disposition of the will—goodwill for people and other creatures. We are enabled to love because God first loved us, and we are called to love as God loves. Indeed, John Wesley observed that the true Christian "loves every man as his own soul. His heart is full of love for all mankind." A Christian's goodwill includes people outside the Christian's family, social network, socio-economic class, nationality, culture, and race. Christians are called to will good for their enemies and even for the enemies of God, because God does.

The Christian is also aware, through the tradition of Jesus, Francis of Assisi, Albert Schweitzer, and others that we are called to revere life and to love the plants and animals because God loves the lily and the sparrow, but we are called to love people even more—because God does. Our calling to love God's creation commits us to ecological causes, to be faithful stewards of creation, and to work with God, and with social movements, to restore creation to health.

The mandate to love people also commits us to the pursuit of Justice. Working for justice is how we love neighbors who are not our neighbors. While love cares for the victims of, say, the wrecks on a mountain highway, justice erects a railing to prevent more people from becoming victims. Working for justice is one way that we join God in answering the prayer "Your will be done, on earth as it is in heaven."

First-generation Christians often report that they are less selfish and less self-centered now. Some report a new capacity to love people that are different from them; some report a deeper capacity to love those closest to them—like a spouse, or a child, or a parent. Some discover a new compassion for neighbors in need, or for oppressed peoples in far-off places, or for abused animals and endangered species.

The third feature of our new life is a **freedom** in Christ—a theme that introduces the remarkable "wideness of God's mercy." The central event of the Old Testament, the Exodus, involves God's liberation of the Hebrew people from bondage in Egypt. The central event of the New Testament, the resurrection of Jesus, involves the liberation of people of faith from the power of death. Furthermore, Paul saw that Jesus Christ sets us free from what Luther called the "tyranny of the Law," i.e., the legalistic trap in which we try to justify our lives to God by obeying all the "rules." For Paul, and Wesley after him, Jesus Christ sets us free from the power of sin. While it is still possible for us to sin, we can be freed from the compulsion to sin. Again, the Church's *Christus Victor* theme, from New Testament times through the Middle Ages, saw Christ's atonement on a cross as liberating us from the power of the Evil One.

When first-generation believers are asked, "What is there in your life that it takes Jesus Christ to explain?" a majority report (among other things) their freedom from something. When they are asked more specifically, "From what, if anything, did Christ set you free?" virtually all of them report one or more liberating experiences connected with becoming a follower of Christ, and the range of experiences they report is astonishing:

> Some New Christians report being set free, by grace, from a legalistic or moralistic agenda for validating their lives. Others report freedom from the opposite of legalism ("antinomianism"); they are liberated from a rudderless lifestyle in which the person lacks any center outside the self, feels accountable to no one, and is victimized by the tyranny of moods.
>
> Others report liberation from some influence of their peer group, or from an ideology, or from idolatry, or from their culture—such as Western culture's rely-only-on-yourself individualism.

Others report, in God's forgiveness, freedom from the power of guilt. Others report freedom from the power of Sin in their lives; in Charles Wesley's words, God takes away "our bent to sinning."

Other Christians report that Christ set them free from a disease, or from an emotional affliction like anxiety, grief, sorrow, or despair. Others report, in growing numbers, how Christ set them free from low self-esteem, or from grandiose self-esteem, or from volatile self-esteem, or from self-preoccupation.

Others report Christ liberating them from the influence of, or possession by, demonic powers or the Evil One. Other people, in greatly growing numbers, report how the "Higher Power" whom they now know as Christ set them free from alcoholism or some other "drug addiction," or from gambling or some other "process addiction," or from some other compulsion, destructive habit, or life pattern around which their life had become unmanageable.

Others report freedom from the haunting memories of child abuse.

Some report the freedom they experienced when the movement of a Just God dismantled the injustice in which they had lived. Others report a spiritual freedom that permitted them to live above their unjust conditions, and even love their enemies.

Still others report that, now that they have become Easter People, they have been set free from their fear of the future and from "the terror of death."

In discovering the freedom to love people as God loves, some new Christians report freedom from self-centeredness, or envy, or jealousy, or hatred, or prejudice. In discovering the freedom to will what God wills, some report freedom from selfishness, and from the need to be controlling.

Most new Christians report that they have not fully appropriated their new freedom in Christ, and they are not yet fully the people God intends them to become. They live between the "no longer" and the "not yet." They are no longer the people they used to be, and not yet the people they are meant to be. But nearly all first generation Christians experience, in some way or ways, their new life as freedom.

The New Lifestyle

The fourth row has four pins, and the first three identify features in the new lifestyle that faith, freedom, love, and obedience make possible.

The first lifestyle pin reminds us that we are called to **live in the world, but not of it.** That is, we are called to live by Kingdom values, rather than

51

the values of Hollywood, or Madison Avenue, or the ideologies in our culture. Wesley explained that the faithful Christian does not let the idols of this world distract her, nor keep the Christian from running her race. "Vice, even if it is fashionable, is still vice." The Christian does not "follow the crowd," and is thereby liberated from the tyranny of the peer group and from the culture's synthetic fads and fashions. Such a Christian does "not lay up treasure on the earth," but rather focuses on "whatever is pure, whatever is pleasing" and so on. Christianity, in other words, involves the redemption of the Christian's attention and consciousness, and clarifies what we live for.

The second pin calls us to a lifestyle of **service and ministry.** We now join a movement that, Wesley said, "does good to all people." So, we feed hungry people, and clothe naked people, and visit sick and imprisoned people. We live no longer for ourselves, but for others. Furthermore, as we discover our spiritual gifts for ministry and begin exercising those gifts, we experience the power of God acting through our ministry.

The third pin calls us to a lifestyle of **witness and mission.** Wesley taught that as the Christian does good to people's bodies, "much more does he labor to do good to their souls." This mission gains in importance because, due to secularization, the Western world is a mission field once again. Jesus taught us to "let [our] light shine before others" and he gave us the Great Commission, so we know that every person has the inalienable right to discover that he or she matters to God, to have the opportunity to covenant with God and with God's People, to experience the new life and live the new lifestyle. Most Christians are best at sharing the good news locally, through their social network of family, friends, neighbors, and fellow workers. But all Christians also have a stake in Christianity's global mission. While there are still some 12,000 unreached people groups across the earth, we are all called to back the world mission of the Christian faith; many are called to give seasons of our lives cross-culturally; some are called to full-time mission careers.

The New Identity

The fourth pin on the fourth row affirms that, as followers of Jesus Christ, **we discover our identity** and we begin to become our true selves. As Wesley emphasized, the image of God is restored within us. If the leading edge of the gospel is that "we matter to God," the "trailing edge" of the gospel is that Jesus Christ has come to make it possible for each of us to become, in this life, the people we were born to be, conceived to be, and deeply within us have always wanted to be. The apostolic congregations all have this goal for people in mind, phrased in one way or another. For instance, Dieter Zander reported that, at New Song Church, "we reminded ourselves continually that we are about helping people become all God meant them to be."

This part of the gospel comes as surprising news to many secular people because, from some church people, non-Christians get the unfortunate message that to become a Christian is to slip on a straitjacket, to lose your individuality, and to become someone you wouldn't want to be. In the early 1970s, when I was teaching at Southern Methodist University's Perkins School of Theology, we still had some students who had entered seminary eluding the Vietnam War. One fellow enrolled in my evangelism course because it was scheduled late enough for him to sleep in! One day, he found me in my office and, as we visited, he shared a surprising confession: "You should know, Mr. Hunter, that I am not a Christian. I believe that Jesus was God's Son, and is God's supreme revelation, and was raised from death— and all that, but I have never invited his spirit into my heart and I don't follow him as Lord of my life."

I asked, "Why? Why?"

"Because I learned in my town in East Texas that if you really open up to Jesus—he twists you into some kind of religious fanatic, or a kook, or somebody you really wouldn't want to be."

I held him by the shoulders and looked into his eyes, saying, "Look, it just isn't so, and somebody back home once sold you a tragic bill of goods. If you could look into the future and see the man that Christ has in mind for you to be ten years from now, you would stand up and cheer and you would deeply want to be that man. The gospel is not bad news; it is good news. The gospel is congruent with our deepest aspirations for ourselves." He said nothing more. He left my office in total silence. Late that night in his dormitory room he sensed Christ approaching him. He took the leap of faith; he was turned inside out.

How Do We Become the People We Were Born to Be?

How does this happen, that in Christ we become our true selves? Some honest mystery is involved that transcends our theories. Furthermore, my interviews with over a thousand first generation Christians have taught me that every person's "experience" is at least somewhat different from every-one else's who ever lived, because each of us is unique. Our souls are at least as unique as our fingerprints, so Jesus Christ extends his own principle of Incarnation and relates to each of us in terms of our particular personality, needs, and history. But at least two features seem to be common to every person's new birth.

Several years ago, I discovered an analogy for one of these features. Lawrence Lacour and his wife, Mildred, came through Lexington and invited my wife, Ella Fay, and me to spend an evening with them. Lawrence Lacour is a splendid senior Methodist evangelist and professor, who, among his many other virtues, is charming, suave, debonair, and sophisticated. It was a serious mistake to let my wife meet him. She started asking me, "Why aren't you charming, suave, debonair, and sophisticated like Lawrence Lacour?" One day I finally replied: "Because his wife brings out the best that is within him!" God is like Mildred Lacour. God relates to us in a way that brings out the best from within us. Our redemption completes our creation.

But another factor also operates in our experience. God also revives, or restores, or even resurrects what was once within us. In her hymn "Rescue the Perishing," Fanny Crosby rejoiced that

> down in the human heart, crushed by the tempter,
> feelings lie buried that grace can restore;
> touched by a loving heart, wakened by kindness,
> chords that were broken will vibrate once more.

I have discovered all ten of these goals for people in the apostolic congregations I have studied, though I have not yet seen all ten emphasized in any one such congregation, and traditional churches may indeed feature one or another. In any case, this is my major discovery: To motivate its people for outreach, and to be effective in outreach, a church must conceive and then communicate a viable model of the kind of Christian our Lord has in mind, that his gospel, his Spirit, and his community make possible. Perhaps a "bowling" model can advance your thinking. In any case, develop a lucid, biblical, relevant model that you can go with and people can grow with. Teach your members, new believers, and seekers what we believe God has in mind for all people. People are more likely to hit the pins if they can see them! Believers are more likely to invite secular pagans to new relationships and a new life than to some variant of the more antiseptic model of traditionalist "churchianity."

CHAPTER THREE

✚

A Case for the Culturally Relevant Congregation

Ι asked several of the Church on Brady's leaders, "How do you reach so many people, when most of the other urban neighborhood churches in your area struggle to survive?" Tom Wolf commented, "You do it here like on any other mission field in the world. Indigenous Christianity engages the population you want to reach. That means using language they understand, and adapting to their cultural style in all the ways you can." Carol Davis added, "Music is crucial. You get the kind of people you offer music for."

That answer is not surprising from a pastor with a degree in Mission from Fuller, and from a church that sends more missionaries than any other Southern Baptist church in the U.S.A. I found, however, that all the leaders of apostolic congregations have a similar perspective. They all take the local culture(s) seriously; they all adapt to the target culture. Today, of course, many church leaders drop the word "culture" as a conversation buzzword; but apostolic congregation leaders were considering culture—and understanding some of its dynamics—in the 1970s.

For instance, when John Ed Mathison moved to Frazer Memorial United Methodist Church in 1972, he perceived that the church had to become much more "indigenous." He studied the relevant 1970 census data, he made a "windshield" survey of the eastern region of Montgomery, he interviewed unchurched people and community leaders, he became involved in the life of the city. He concluded that their strategy had to be "homegrown"—not imported from another context—and their ministries had to fit the needs and culture of the people they wanted to reach. He moved the church into "informal celebrative" worship featuring "music that unchurched folks can relate to. I would rather have a volunteer choir singing something that unchurched folks can relate to than pay ten professional artists to sing something in Latin that nobody understands!"

55

The Vineyard movement was conceived, and has spread, with this "missiological" understanding. So, one of the published values of Cincinnati's Vineyard Community Church reads: "We value being culture current. We reflect this through worship music that is of a popular style. We aim to develop an atmosphere of ease to speak, act, and dress in ways in which 'baby boomers' can readily respond positively."

Rick Warren began Saddleback Valley Community Church by taking a personal survey of the unchurched population in their targeted region of Orange County, California. Gradually, the data was shaped into a profile of "Saddleback Sam": the church's mission is to reach people like him. Warren observes that "most churches have people blindness. They try to treat all people the same, but they are not all the same." Warren and other apostolic pastors believe that the communicating pastor and church must learn to "exegete" the "context" as well as the "text" in order to communicate the meaning of the text to the target population in their cultural context.

Cultural relevance may be the most important, the most controversial, and the most difficult of an apostolic congregation's features to introduce into the life of a traditional congregation. One reason for the controversy and difficulty is that it typically becomes an integrity issue. Traditional churches usually assume that cultural integrity requires them to perpetuate the cultural forms that God blessed in the past, often in a movement's European past, rather than adapting to the forms of today's target population. Or they assume that cultural integrity requires them to import the "best" cultural forms, especially classical music, from the Christian tradition. In missiology, however, we have become convinced that gospel integrity calls us to cultural flexibility. I have observed that apostolic church leaders usually think their way toward an indigenous strategy by identifying and empathizing with the experiences of unchurched pre-Christians. So we begin our Case with a case.

How Secular People Experience
Traditional Congregations

One Saturday evening, Dave said to his girlfriend Jennifer, "Let's go to church tomorrow morning." Jennifer knew that the tip of an iceberg had just surfaced. Dave had tried football and fraternity life, alcohol and astrology, New Age and nude therapy, several drugs and several marriages in a driven twelve-year quest to make sense of his life, get his act together, "grab the gusto," experience life to the fullest, and find something worth living for. Until an injury, vertical rock climbing had given him an adrenaline rush—which was the nearest he had experienced to really living. Every idol had promised more than it delivered. Somewhere, he had heard, "If you have tried everything else, you might try God," and, "the place to try God is at a church on a Sunday morning."

Jennifer agreed, and a search in the Yellow Pages revealed several churches on the highway that Dave and Jennifer both took to work each day—to the regional insurance office where he worked as a claims processor, and to the county courthouse where she worked as a court reporter. A half-dozen churches each featured a service around eleven o'clock. Dave had no church background; he couldn't even tell you the name of the church his parents had stayed away from until their divorce, when Dave was about 14. Jennifer had been raised a nominal United Methodist, and had even "graduated" from a confirmation class, so they decided to visit a United Methodist Church. They experienced the United Methodist service as bizarre. The music, the liturgy, the language, and the whole ethos reeked of the 1950s—an era when kids entered yo-yo tournaments, when Milton Berle, Ed Sullivan, and Lucille Ball dominated America's black-and-white television sets, when people drove Studebakers, Kaisers, Frazers, Desotos, and Hudsons, and the Volkswagen Beetle was new in America. Most of the people were older and upper middle class; Jennifer noticed several mink coats, but no Bibles. The liturgical leaders conducted the service at a pre-Elvis pace, with massive dead spots when nothing was happening except for organ interludes. Dave got acutely in touch with something his grapevine occasionally reported: that Christianity is "boring." The sermon might have rescued this experience, but the thirty-minute lecture that promoted "justice issues" (such as saving the peregrine falcon and ordaining homosexuals) did not become a medium of God's Living Word for Jennifer or Dave.

They visited an Independent Baptist church the next Sunday and had a very different experience. The people were blue-collar. The church's use of English seemed affected, as testimonies and the sermon referred to "sein," "Gawd," and "Chriiist." The hymns contained countless allusions to biblical characters, verses, and themes that were not already within Dave and Jennifer's memory bank. The sermon, which preached divine judgment against homosexuality, pornography, high taxes, and Bill Clinton (and against the United Methodist church down the street) failed to engage any of Dave and Jennifer's needs and violated the code of "tolerance" which is so important to their generation.

They tried a Nazarene church, and could not fathom why the church made such a big deal about women's makeup; Dave was frightened to think that maybe that is what is important to God! They visited an Episcopal church, but could not relate to the Elizabethan language, the European pipe organ music, and the Latin anthem. They visited an Evangelical Covenant church, but didn't feel as Scandinavian as the members. They visited a Lutheran church and didn't feel that German either.

Dave and Jennifer visited a half-dozen churches within a two-month period. They were all different, yet Jennifer and (especially) Dave experienced them similarly—as congregations of people they could not identify with, with messages not relevant to their needs and questions, and (particularly) as places culturally alien to people like Dave and Jennifer. So they tentatively concluded that God is not for people like them.

Jennifer and Dave have experienced the most widespread, entrenched, and formidable barrier that prevents the most people from considering the Christian faith today: the "culture barrier." Traditional evangelical churches and traditional liberal churches both erect and maintain their own versions of this barrier, however unwittingly, and they thereby block people, including many serious seekers, from faith.

The Current Rise of "Apostolic Congregations"

However, the "apostolic congregations" that are emerging over the land are more different from the traditional churches on this point than any other. As once the apostle Paul was willing to "become all things to all people that [he] might by all means save some," so **we are observing the emergence of entire congregations who are willing to be culturally flexible in order to reach people.** These churches are dramatizing a truth that missionaries have known for decades: To reach non-Christian populations, it is necessary for a church to become culturally indigenous to its "mission field"—whether that field is in Asia, Africa, Latin America, or Oceania, or in Europe or North America. When a church employs the language, music, style, architecture, art forms, and other forms of the target population's culture, Christianity then has a fair chance to become contagious within their ranks. But when the church's communication forms are alien to the host population, they may never perceive that Christianity's God is for people like them.

Other Barriers to Faith

The "culture barrier" is not, of course, the only barrier that keeps people from faith. Interviews with secular people reveal other barriers. For example, around the credibility issue, the church historically has been wrong so many times on issues concerning science and human freedom that secular people question its intellectual credibility.

Many secular people also question the life credibility of professing Christians. Some of them think we don't really believe it. Some think we believe it, but we don't live it. Still others think we live it and believe it, but it really doesn't make much difference!

Some secular people are turned off by the Church's image. They often think the Church represents only an inherited folk wisdom one-half a cut above the level of, say, the *Farmer's Almanac*. Or they think of the Church as irrelevant, okay for little children and "the little old ladies of both sexes," but "it doesn't scratch where we itch." Or they think of church as "boring"—offering dusty old hymns, liturgies that drag, and boring sermons that endorse a plain vanilla, rule-bound, "Christian life" devoid of adventure.

Furthermore, some barriers are within the spirit of the secular seeker. Some love their sins more than they want to love God. Some want their agenda more than God's agenda. The souls of many people are affixed for now to some idol, and their hearts are hardened and not open to the gospel's appeal.

The Culture Barrier

The largest and most widespread barrier (that we have any control over) that keeps people from faith is the culture barrier. In interviews with secular people, I often ask, "What keeps people like you from considering the Christian faith?" At least three out of four unchurched people refer to this barrier, among others. When Christian converts are asked, "What almost kept you from becoming involved with the Christian faith?" over half of our converts refer to this barrier. People phrase this barrier in many ways, but we can state its essence in one sentence: **They resist becoming Christians because they "don't want to become like church people"**—which they believe is a prerequisite for becoming a Christian.

When unchurched pre-Christian people talk about "church people," unfortunately they do not refer to people who transparently love God and their neighbors, who serve the community and live for others. Something in the church's "body language" shouts more loudly than the new life and the new lifestyle embodied in some of the members. Unchurched people are struck first, and put off, by the dated or alien church subculture. For example, they are alienated when they overhear church people using an "alien language" or a "pious jargon." The "jargon" problem cuts several ways, and the technical jargon of desk theologians, the revival jargon of the late–nineteenth century, and the "politically correct" jargon of the late–twentieth century all have similar alienating effects. Pre-Christians also notice that church people have antiquated, or even foreign, tastes in music, art, and architecture, that they love their traditions more than they love the surrounding community, and that they dress and act in "abnormal" ways.

59

So, non-Christians typically experience the Church as a distinct subculture with its own values, customs, norms, habits, language, music, aesthetics, and so on, and they think that you have to think, talk, dress, and act "that way," and learn to enjoy, for example, eighteenth-century German pipe organ music before you can become a Christian! They suspect that the Church's agenda is to change other people *culturally*. Let me quote several such people: "Christians live in their own little world, in their private pious cliques, with their buzzwords and their prescribed behaviors." "What do church people mean when they sing about being 'washed in the blood,' or 'dwelling in Beulah Land'?" "What are they doing when they are raising their 'Ebenezer'?" "What does it look like when 'angels prostrate fall'? " "Why are Christians always synthetically polite?" One new Christian reports, "I loathed the possibility of becoming like nice sociable church people going through the motions. The thought made me ill." The problem they experience, and avoid, is that churches seem to require people to "become like us" before they will be regarded and included as real Christians. We have thus rediscovered Donald McGavran's observation that the barriers that keep most people from faith and discipleship are more cultural and sociological than theological or religious.

The Culture Barrier in Church History

Let me attempt to put this problem in some perspective. The Church has seemed to require people to "become like us" culturally for a very long time. We find this pattern as early as the history recorded in Acts 15. The early church in Jerusalem was requiring their Gentile converts to become circumcised, give up pork, obey Sabbath laws and other rules and regulations, and become culturally Jewish as a requirement for becoming baptized followers of Jesus the Messiah.[1] Meanwhile, up in Antioch, Gentiles were becoming disciples in great numbers and were not also becoming "kosher." This precipitated a crisis at the Jerusalem "headquarters" of the young Christian movement, and occasioned "The Jerusalem Council" that is reported in Acts 15. After the parties of James, Paul, and Simon Peter deliberated the issue, the council determined that Gentiles did not have to become culturally kosher to follow Christ and be part of his movement.

The Jerusalem Council's decision was momentous. Without that decision, Christianity might have remained a sect of "fulfilled Jews" within Judaism. The decision extended the principle of Incarnation; as Jesus had adapted to Galilean Aramaic-speaking peasant culture, so the Church, his Body, could now become "indigenous" to all the cultures of the earth.[2] Now that Gentiles did not have to become Jews to become Christians, the faith was unleashed to spread and adapt within three centuries to most of the major cultures in the Roman Empire, and to later become the world's most universal faith.

It would seem that the Jerusalem Council settled a very significant matter, and it did. But Christianity has struggled with the problem, in many versions, ever since. In the years following the Jerusalem Council, the party of James (the "Judaizers") reverted to Plan A and decided that Jewish enculturation was a necessary part of Christian discipleship after all. The Judaizers even grew for awhile, and they fanned out across the Mediterranean world—stirring up people in several churches Paul had planted, prompting several letters from Paul, notably his Letter to the Galatians.

In one way, at least, the party of Paul failed to fully implement the Jerusalem Council's decision. The Christian movement became predominantly Gentile, and throughout most of our history Jewish people have not become Christians—in part because they felt required to become culturally Gentile as a prerequisite to becoming Christians! Only in the last quarter century has the church enabled a *Jewish* Christian movement, employing the cultural forms of Jews to reach and nurture Jews. Consequently, through Jews For Jesus and the Messianic Synagogue movement, an unprecedented number of Jews have become fulfilled Jews.

As the Christian faith spread across much of the earth, the earth's peoples often experienced it to require some equivalent to circumcision. Indeed, the Church often expected the peoples of Asia, Africa, Latin America, and Oceania to become "Westernized" as a part of, often as a prerequisite to, being "Christianized." Until Vatican II, for example, the Roman Catholic Church required that the mass be held in Latin everywhere. Protestant mission has usually been friendlier to vernacular languages, but has often assumed that people could not become Christians without becoming "civilized" first—by a Western model!

We now know that Western nations have no monopoly on "cultural imperialism." For instance, South Korean churches are now sending out hundreds of missionaries to other lands and peoples. Seoul Theological Seminary has established a School of World Mission—to better prepare missionaries, because they discovered that Korean missionaries were planting culturally Korean churches from Thailand to Zambia! So, the indigenizing principle was established in the Council at Jerusalem, but its implementation does not come automatically for any of us. The culture in which any of us are raised seems "natural" to us, so we would naturally extend "our kind" of Christianity everywhere unless we know how important it is to adapt to other cultures.

The Culture Barrier Today

The culture barrier between the churches and the unchurched people of Europe is the largest single cause of European Christianity's decline in this century. Martin Robinson's recent book *A World Apart* reports that Great Britain's thousands of Protestant chapels, which once fit British culture and engaged great numbers of people, have not changed as British culture has changed, with this result:

> Visitors to such chapels can see all too easily the yawning chasm between what takes place in the culture of chapel life and the culture of those who live in the neighborhood. It is as if the chapel folk are silently saying to the community: "To become a Christian, you not only have to believe that Jesus Christ was the Son of God, that he died on a cross and was raised from the dead on the third day; you also have to find a way of living in a culture that no longer exists in everyday life."[3]

Robinson also observes that the Church's "cultural blindness" prevents it from even perceiving "the distinction between the gospel and the cultural forms in which we express it," and that fact "is responsible for a great deal of the failure of the church to make a significant impact on the society of which we are a part."[4]

The culture barrier is an even bigger problem for mainline American Christianity, because we bought the early-twentieth-century myth of the "American Melting Pot." That myth taught that people come from the nations of the other continents and enter a "melting pot" experience in which everyone comes out as assimilated mainline Americans. But the myth really assumed a more imperialistic process—that people who come from the earth's various nations should become like those of us whose ancestors came from Great Britain! So American Christianity has added to the usual expectations that the people who join our churches will become "like us." But with the rise of what Michael Novak called "the unmeltable ethnics," we observe people of many cultures and subcultures whose culture seems as "natural" to them as ours does to us, who like their art, music, style, and language (or dialect) about as much as we like ours, who are not motivated to "become circumcised" and become like us.

My suggestion that cultural imperialism afflicts the churches of America may, of course, be met with denial, because this is virtually no one's conscious intention. Are America's church people the North American "Judaizers"? Do we really expect people to become "like us"? Do outsiders really perceive us as requiring that?

Let's ask our own youth—who, since the 1950s, have developed their own subculture, with its own distinct (and evolving) norms for clothing and hair styles, with its own jargon and dance and music. In this forty-year period, youth ministry has declined as a priority within most mainline denominations, and the number of youth in our churches today is less than half of what it was forty years ago. The Church, generally, has failed to adapt to the developing subculture of young people or to take seriously their concerns and causes. Furthermore, our teenagers and young adults are no more likely to adapt to churches perpetuating the 1950s than they are likely to buy their father's Oldsmobile.

Do we Christians seem to require people to become like us? Let's ask the American peoples of non-Anglo races and cultures. For years we have heard that the most segregated hour of the week is eleven to twelve on Sunday morning; we repented and made the achievement of integrated congregations the de facto priority in my denomination and many others. We were unable to achieve it. Why? The way the objective was often phrased gives a clue: We wanted African Americans and others "to join our churches." Ethnic minority people *visited* "our churches" in those years, but they seldom came back and almost never joined. We seemed to be requiring them to become culturally Anglo, "like us." They resisted their "ethnocide," i.e., the elimination of their culture by being absorbed into ours.

If you harbor doubts about this reading of our history, I invite contrary evidence: When did any Anglo congregations say to African American visitors, "We will change to an African American style of music?" When did any Anglo congregation say to Hispanic visitors, "We will conduct the worship service in Spanish?" When did the denomination say to ordination candidates from Korea or the Caribbean, "We will ordain you on the basis of your denomination's ordination standards in the land you came from"? Peter Wagner's tough phrase is all too accurate: mainline American Christianity has followed, usually unconsciously, a policy of "assimilationist racism."[5]

Let's ask ourselves some painfully specific questions. How open are we to people who drink, or smoke? How open are we to "hard living" people with addictions and soap opera values? How open are we to young men who ride motorcycles, who wear jeans, long hair, left earrings, and leather jackets with the words "Life Sucks." How open are we, really, to illiterate people, to homeless people, to people with AIDS? How open are we to people with dirt under their fingernails, or unshined shoes, with bad breath or body odor, who might belch or break wind or split an infinitive in the church building?

Such questions are important because the U.S. has tens of millions of people who have some "rough edges," who lack some middle-class social graces, who can't read music and wouldn't know how to second a motion, who aren't quite "refined," who lack many of the "civilized" standards of church people. Our Church subculture has erected dozens of barriers that separate many people from the possibility of becoming disciples. Virtually all of these barriers are essentially cultural barriers, and have little or nothing to do with "the faith once delivered to the saints."

Theological Perspectives for Removing the Culture Barrier

There is a solution to the culture barrier. Two very important theological affirmations need to guide our way.

First, at the deep worldview level of culture, Christians have a distinct view of ultimate reality—that what we believe is revealed by God in history, supremely in Christ, and attested in Scripture. As David Burnett has shown, in *Clash of Worlds*, the distinctive view of reality we see through biblical lenses can be readily demonstrated in the anthropologist's categories of cosmos, self, knowing, community, time, and value.[6]

For example, in our view of the cosmos, we Christians believe in a "triune" God, who has characteristics of holiness, power, and love, whose creation is "good," distinct from God, consists of both material and spiritual realms, and is the theater of God's action. In our view of the Self, we believe that people are created in God's image, are distinct from other creatures, are intended for a covenantal relationship with God, and are to live for God's moral purposes in the world—including the stewardship of creation—but we are sinners in need of forgiveness, reconciliation, and restoration.

We can "know" the Truth primarily from God's self-revelation to us, and also from reasonable thought, reflection upon our experiences, and from the cumulative experience and reflection of the faith community. We are social beings, with a need for community—with all people at one level, and in the messianic community at a deeper level. We understand time as beginning with creation and anticipating the consummation of God's promised Kingdom, and we cooperate with God's revealed will in time. From just that much, we can see that the Christian worldview is unique among the major religions, philosophies, and ideologies of the earth.

Quite apart from the anthropologist's grid, we are aware of Christianity's unique deep-level culture, with its unique Story, stories, and symbols, with its distinct history, heroes, meanings, values, and rituals. As a specific example, the Christian funeral gives its people permission and reason to both grieve and celebrate. Furthermore, we all know that each denomination gives its people membership in a specific Christian subculture, with its own deep insights and integrity.

This is the point: In our mission, we are not called to surrender or compromise this way in which Christians perceive reality. Indeed, Christ

64

commissions us to communicate our most central truth claims to people who do not yet wear New Testament lenses, knowing that Christian conversion involves (in part) the putting on of those lenses and the transformation of one's worldview. The Truth is not negotiable.

But the outer forms through which the Truth is communicated are negotiable, and that is the second major insight that should guide our way. To reach an undiscipled population, the forms of outreach, ministry, and worship must be indigenous to their culture, because each people's culture is the natural medium of God's revelation to them.

So the Church can choose to cooperate with the Acts 15 decision and develop what missiologists call "culturally indigenous churches" in this mission field as we do in other fields. We can start Sunday school classes, house groups, worship services, and new congregations that fit the cultures of the various unchurched populations in North America. We can choose to use language and music they understand and can relate to. We can encourage clothing and styles they are comfortable with. We can minister to their felt needs and their struggles. The U.S. is a vast secular mission field, with many cultures and subcultures. Are we imaginative enough and compassionate enough to sponsor and unleash many forms of indigenous Christianity in this land?

Several additional theological insights can ground and guide a more indigenous strategy:

• Jesus came and adapted to a specific culture—Galilean peasant Jewish culture, speaking a "hillbilly" (Aramaic) Hebrew dialect. He calls his Church to follow in his steps and extend his Incarnation into every specific culture on earth—so that every people will perceive that the Triune God of the Christian faith is for people like them.
• A saving revelation of God is possible in any culture. Every culture has enough to work with and the Holy Spirit makes up the difference, so the meaning of the Christian gospel can be communicated in any culture. (If you doubt this claim, recall that God's original revelation did not come to Anglo people in the U.S. What we have in Anglo-American Christianity is a cultural adaptation of original biblical Christianity; if we got the meaning through our cultural forms then, presumably, so can any other society.)
• We have received the gospel treasure in "earthen vessels," but we often mistake the vessel for the treasure; then we confuse faithfulness to the gospel with perpetuating and extending the cultural forms in which we received it! Instead, we are called to unwrap the gospel's meaning from the cultural forms in which we received it and rewrap it in the cultural forms of the target population.

- We believe that, as Jesus came "not to destroy" Jewish law, tradition, and culture, "but to fulfill them," so he came not to destroy but to fulfill all the earth's cultures.
- This principle calls the indigenous Christians in each society to function in their society as "salt"—preserving everything in their culture that is possible within God's will, and as "light"—changing what is necessary.
- This strategy would align the Christian movement with the basic apostolic principles modeled by Paul—who communicated everywhere the one gospel of "Jesus Christ and him crucified," but communicated this gospel by being "all things to all people that I might by all means save some."

Reflecting this apostolic perspective, the Lausanne movement's *Willowbank Report* declares that "no Christian witness can hope to communicate the gospel if he or she ignores the cultural factor."[7] A faithful strategy calls "us" to adapt to "their" culture and does not require them to "become kosher" and adopt our culture.

Historical Precedents for Removing the Culture Barrier

Fortunately, we do not need to consider this principle merely as an abstraction. Martin Luther pioneered the principle in earliest Protestant Christianity—by abandoning the Latin Bible and mass. Luther translated the Scriptures into the vernacular German language of the people he served, and Lutheran churches worshiped in German and developed a German hymnody employing the (then) contemporary folk music, and even the beer hall music, that the German people already knew and loved. Luther's purpose was to communicate the message of Scripture through the people's music.[8]

The Methodist heritage extended the indigenous principle. John and Charles Wesley led their apostolic movement by adapting to eighteenth-century British culture. They "agreed to become more vile" and preached in the fields and town squares—on the unchurched people's turf. They wrote Christian poetry to be sung to the tunes the people knew and loved to sing in the public houses. They created an architectural style for chapels in which common people would be comfortable. They coached Methodists to speak in "the most obvious, easy, common words, wherein our meaning can be conveyed" and to "never . . . deviate from the most usual way of speaking."[9] A century later, General William Booth, founder of the Salvation Army, asked, "Why should the Devil have all the good tunes?" and introduced urban streets to Christian band music in the popular genre of nineteenth-century Britain.

Three Options for Church Leaders Today

Over time, the tastes and styles of cultures change, so that words, music, attire, or style that once fit the culture is later experienced as "old-fashioned" or even "alien." Consequently, most unchurched people today are no longer culturally shaped to resonate to the music of the harpsichord or the pipe organ, or to relate to the music of Bach, Beethoven, or Handel, or the hymns of Martin Luther, or Charles Wesley, or Fanny Crosby, or traditional Salvation Army band music.

What are the Church's options as it reflects upon its mission in a changed culture? Church leaders, typically, have responded in one of three ways:

- Often, the leaders have unnecessarily bonded the gospel treasure to the cultural forms that were employed in the past when the movement was most successful. They assume that the mission must perpetuate those forms and, if the target population does not respond to our inherited cultural forms, they are rejecting the gospel.
- Often, some elitists (usually "high church" musicians) impose foreign forms upon the church—to "raise" the cultural aesthetics of Christians and non-Christians. The elitists really do believe that everyone would be "better" if they were force-fed eighteenth-century pipe organ music! When people, Christians and non-Christians, are exposed to such cultural imperialism—they usually vote with their feet, by absentee ballot!
- The most faithful and effective option, I suggest, is to recover the vision and imagination of our founding geniuses, to "exegete" the culture God entrusts to us—as they did in theirs, and to "indigenize" the faith's language, music, and style once again. We do not honor our founders by blindly perpetuating in a changing world what they once did, nor by hijacking their tradition and imposing something culturally alien; we honor them by doing for our time and culture what they did for theirs.

Fortunately, most of our churches have already discovered one of the two crucial insights, and have already taken the first of two giant steps required to implement the third option. We have known, and owned, that communication must be in the general language of the people. So, when immigrants came from Germany, Sweden, Korea, Mexico, or Haiti, most denominations knew to offer ministries in German, Swedish, Korean, Spanish, or Creole. Furthermore, many Christian traditions already know that as a people's language changes (from, say, Swedish to English or from the grandparent's English to current English), the language employed in ministry should change. So, while a few extreme traditionalists hold out for the King James Bible and for *thee* and *thou* in their liturgy, most churches *at least* use post–Elizabethan English and twentieth-century translations of the Bible.

Most churches, however, still need to discover the second crucial insight and take a second giant step. They need to discover that **culture** is "the silent language." As Edward T. Hall demonstrated in cultural anthropology classics like *The Silent Language* and *Beyond Culture,* communication depends as much upon cultural factors as upon language factors. Furthermore, people experience the effects of cultural factors more unconsciously than the effects of language factors, because they learned their language rather consciously but they "acquired" their culture rather unconsciously. (So, if you use a word beyond someone's vocabulary, they will know why they feel intimidated; if you stand closer to them than they are culturally conditioned to feel is normal, they may not know why they feel intimidated.) Consequently, people live out much of their life rather unconsciously through the observable symbols and customs, and the deeper "map" of reality, programmed into them by their enculturation. For this reason, the gospel is communicated through a people's language *and* their art, architecture, music, communication patterns, "body language," leadership style, and so on. The remaining giant step to take, based upon this insight, is to make *all* of the forms in which we communicate the meanings of Christianity, not just the language, culturally appropriate to the population we are called to serve and reach.

If we harbor any lingering doubts about the need for the second step, we may need to look no farther to validate the principle than ourselves. If we are honest, we will admit that there are, say, some kinds of music, some forms of art, some clothing, and hair, and leadership styles, and some dialects or accents of our own language that turn us off, or at least do not appeal to us, or are not "natural" to us. Go ahead, pick an accent or type of music you do not particularly like. In the period when you became a Christian, if Christianity had been offered to you only in that accent and celebrated only through that music, would you as likely be a Christian today? The point is little more profound than this: Most people out there are like you and me! The Christian faith will be more effectively communicated, understood, and adopted by every population through forms that are culturally appropriate to them.

The (Re)Emergence of the "Seekers' Service"

Many Protestant churches and traditions offered worship services targeting (and tailored for) pre-Christians for over 150 years. They were called "Gospel Services," or "Evangelistic Services," or simply the "Sunday Evening Service." The social contract was once clear to everyone: the Sunday morning service was primarily for Christians, the Sunday evening service was primarily for pre-Christian people. The early pioneers of Sunday evening services brought vision and imagination to this daring innovation—a worship service primarily for people who were not yet disciples! Throughout its noble history, the Sunday evening service was more informal and "user-friendly"; it employed the people's language, and more enjoyable, singable, and (then) indigenous music; the preaching bridged human needs and gospel explanation; the people prayed, the Spirit visited, and people experienced forgiveness, faith, healing, empowerment, visions, and perhaps a call to serve the mission of Christ in some distant land.

With some differences by region and culture, the Sunday evening service thrived for several generations, and then declined in attendance and vitality. One reason for its decline is that the culture around the church changed, but the Sunday evening liturgy, language, and music did not. Church leaders perpetuated what was now the "old evangelistic" approach; they were sure that the same God who blessed people through it in the past would do it in the present and the future—if only the current generation of Christians were more supportive, or more spiritual, or tried harder. The methods that once gathered great harvests later yielded diminishing harvests and, in time, virtually no harvest. Most churches eventually abandoned the Sunday evening service without replacing it with anything else for catalyzing regular outreach.

Throughout this history, other churches did not offer a Sunday evening evangelistic service. These pastors and churches tended to be from the more liturgical or "scholarly" traditions. They sometimes criticized the Sunday evening service for its "low brow" liturgy, or its aesthetically "inferior" music, or its "emotionalism" or "manipulation." As the Sunday evening service eventually declined in attendance and effectiveness, the criticisms gained plausibility.

Meanwhile, many of the churches perpetuating the Sunday evening tradition slipped into what addiction literature calls a form of "insanity," that is "doing the same thing over and over again, each time expecting a different result!" History did not reverse its course and the old results did not revisit, but the old Sunday evening service was perpetuated—as a demonstration that the pastor and the church were still "evangelical" and had not lost the faith. The service's actual mission had turned, inch by inch, almost 180 degrees. Once the evening service's target audience had been pre-Christian unchurched people. Now the target audience became the members, and the de facto goal now was to preach and pray Christians into a deeper commitment and spiritual life.

The churches still thought of the Sunday evening service as "evangelism," even though conversions were few and seekers no longer came to a church on Sunday evenings. The seekers stopped coming on Sunday evenings roughly at the same rate at which their cultural world changed and the Sunday evening service did not. Over the decades, as they could relate to the service's language, style, and music less and less, they came less and less.

In the 1970s however, a few perceptive church leaders saw secular people showing up at church on Sunday mornings. An enduring maxim in secular Western folk culture says, "If you have tried everything else, you might try God. The place to try God is a church; the time is on Sunday morning." Unchurched people no longer knew, and had not known for decades, that pre-Christian people are not supposed to come on Sunday morning, but on Sunday evening. They saw the most people going to church on Sunday morning, so they began using the Sunday morning service to check out Christianity.

Perceptive church leaders saw visitors like Dave and Jennifer (with whom we began this chapter) not moving their lips during the creed, fumbling to find Second Corinthians in the pew Bible, standing up or sitting down after everyone else, and walking out with confused expressions. These church leaders interviewed, or befriended, some people like Dave and Jennifer, perceived how tragically "church as usual" was missing these pre-Christian visitors, and heard the sad conclusions they often reached from their experience in church: "I can't relate to it," or "Christianity is irrelevant and boring," or "God must not be interested in people like us. If he was, he would speak our language!" They saw that the seeker's pattern of trying to learn about Christianity in a service that was not designed to introduce Christianity was a ludicrous and counterproductive exercise.

Some of these church leaders took pains to find out what kind of language unchurched people understand and the kind of music to which they resonate and, in time, they understood something about secular unchurched people's styles and lifestyles, their needs and values, heroes and role models, struggles and hang-ups, interests and idols. They began imagining what a culturally relevant church would look like, especially at worship.

Robert Schuller was an early pioneer in wanting to understand unchurched people and adapt in ways to become an effective missionary congregation in North America. Though all the pastors and churches featured in this book have moved beyond Schuller and the Crystal Cathedral in their apostolic approach, most of them stand on his shoulders and affirm his important formula:

- The unchurched people's needs will determine our programs.
- The unchurched people's hang-ups will determine our strategy.
- The unchurched people's culture will determine our style.
- The unchurched population will determine our growth goals.

Since the 1970s, thoughtful church leaders who wanted to reach secular seekers responded in one of four ways. The first way is usually unproductive, the other three productive.

The first response began when church leaders attempted a **"blended service"**—a little Bach, Watts, Shea, and (later) Gaither in the same service. For years, that approach appeared to engage most of the members and some outsiders, for the same reasons that the "something for everybody" approach sold *Life, Look,* and *Saturday Evening Post* by the millions. By the 1970s and 1980s however, the culture had changed enough that people abandoned the once-popular smorgasbord magazines in favor of *Cat Fancy, Runner's World, Muscle and Fitness, MacWorld, Longevity, Backpacker, Scuba Diving, Stock Car Racing, Working Woman, Black Enterprise, Soap Opera Magazine* and hundreds of other magazines for very specific "markets." The cultural expectation shifted—from "something for me" to "the whole thing for me!" The responses to worship services have shifted similarly so that, today, a blended service "really provides something for everybody to be unhappy about!"[10]

The second response began spreading in the 1970s when some leaders, like John Ed Mathison and his colleagues at Frazer Memorial United Methodist Church in Montgomery, Alabama developed a **"Seeker Friendly"** worship service—a fairly traditional service (organ, choir, traditional hymns, and so on), but less formal (the pastor wears a sport coat), very celebrative—somewhat like a "low church" pageant, and made very manageable for the uninitiated seeker. In Frazer's three identical Sunday morning services, memorization of the creed is not assumed; it is printed in the bulletin. The bulletin and liturgist announce the page in the pew Bible where people can find the reading in Second Corinthians, or they print the passage in the bulletin. In a couple of dozen ways, the church makes "our worship service" an unintimidating, manageable, friendly journey for people who don't know much about "church."

Third, some leaders like Rick Warren and his colleagues at Saddleback Valley Community Church in Orange County, California developed a **"High Participation Seeker service."** Saddleback features no organ ("and

71

never will!"), but a band; no choir, but singing ensembles. The service is primarily for pre-Christians and somewhat secondarily for Christians, but it targets both. Saddleback's four identical weekend services are informal, even "laid back"; Rick Warren usually speaks in shirtsleeves, often with no necktie. The music features "adult contemporary" songs, praise songs, and choruses (usually no music written before 1980!) and the service, especially the lengthy music portion, is very participatory, and celebrative—somewhat like a rally. The sermon addresses a topic, like "Stress-Busters," "Healthy Self-esteem," "Keeping a Marriage Together," or "Finding a Purpose,"—addressing the topic, in nonreligious language, from the wisdom of one or more relevant biblical texts.

Fourth, some leaders, like Bill Hybels and his colleagues at Willow Creek Community Church in Chicago, have developed a "**High Performance Seeker service**" that they offer once on Saturday evening and twice Sunday morning. There are some similarities between the two types of seeker services: Both target seekers; both feature a band or orchestra, not an organ, and singing ensembles, not a choir; both feature adult contemporary music and topical-biblical preaching in the culture's language. Both types of service attempt to present "Christianity 101" much of the time, and demonstrate Christianity's redemptive relevance to people's needs and struggles.

There are also important dissimilarities between the high participation and the high performance types of seeker services. The high performance service is shaped even more for non-Christians, and even less for Christians. Indeed, Bill Hybels believes that "you cannot, maximally, in the same service, meet the needs of both Christians and non-Christians"; so Willow Creek's distinct service for believers meets Wednesday and Thursday nights. Willow Creek's high performance seeker service is much less participatory than a high participation seeker service or than Willow Creek's believers service. Early in Willow Creek's seeker service, the people sing one song and greet people around them; otherwise, overt congregational participation is minimal—somewhat like a concert or peformance (though, when it "works," the people are inwardly moved and involved). Willow Creek's studies of their target population revealed that many unchurched people "don't want to sing anything, say anything, or sign anything." They want to explore Christianity, anonymously, at their own pace; so Willow Creek is committed to providing "a safe place to consider the dangerous message of Jesus Christ." The service often features a short drama before the message, because Willow Creek's leaders believe that this generation, the first raised on television from infancy, is less capable of processing abstract ideas than previous generations; they need to see it dramatized, like on a TV "sitcom."

Despite my studies of secular people and apostolic congregations, I do not occupy some Olympian vantage point from which I can arbitrate between the seeker friendly, high participation, and high performance approaches and pronounce which one is "right." My interviews with secular people and with converts out of secularity convince me that all three are right, in the sense that each has identified and engaged a distinct type of personality within the secular masses. Some folks, including many Baby Boomers, want a service to be tailored to them, and they need to process the possibility as anonymous spectators—at least for a while; the high performance seeker service is probably best for them. Some people, including many Baby Busters, need to "try it on," or experience it before they can commit, and they say, "Don't sugarcoat it or slant it for us. We want to hear what you tell the Christians." The high participation seeker service is probably best for them. Some people, including many people born before World War II and many people from Roman Catholic or Bible Belt subcultures, expect the service to have roots in the past—but to be accessible. The "seeker friendly" service is probably best for them.

As a practical matter, some church staffs cannot, for the foreseeable future, prepare and deliver with excellence both a seekers service and a different believers service every week. Some churches have been able to staff it, and found that their members perferred the seeker service, leaving the believers service with low attendance. But those who have pulled off both, and brought their people along, swear by it.

Moreover, many secular personalities are sufficiently flexible that they could be reached by either service. The service's faithfulness, clarity, excellence, and relevance, and the leaders' and membership's openness, goodwill, and sense of God's presence are more crucial variables for many seekers than whether they spectate or participate. The small church may have to choose between these options, but the large church may be able to "have it both ways." Rick Warren suggests that the *large* high participation seeker service permits individuals, without feeling conspicuous, merely to observe if they want to.

The Controversy over Contemporary Worship

You now know enough of the vision, rationale, and perspective of the field of "Missiology," and enough of the history and rationale behind the phenomenon of Seekers Services, to work through a volatile issue with which many churches now struggle, although—as you know—the issue is not as "new" as most church leaders assume. The latter two forms of a seeker targeted worship service are both popularly thought of as "Seeker

Services," and the whole approach has become a subject of intense controversy.

You will see that the descendants of the critics of the old Sunday evening service are conforming to their genetic script or ancestral memory. That is important to note, because the Seeker Service is not the radical unprecedented innovation the critics paint it to be. Essentially, apostolic churches have revised, updated, and rescheduled the Sunday evening service for Sunday morning—because that is when the target audience will come! Let's look at a couple of episodes in this controversy, which has generated much more heat than light, because many churches will need to work through the controversy and get past it before they are likely to reach the unchurched.

Walt Kallestad, senior pastor of The Community Church of Joy, wrote a one-page article entitled "Entertainment Evangelism" in a 1990 issue of his denomination's periodical *The Lutheran.* In his first paragraph, Kallestad declared: "It is time for the Christian church to become serious about penetrating the heart of the culture with the heart of the gospel." Furthermore, he argued that Sunday morning is now the optimum time to involve "the 60 percent to 90 percent unchurched unreached population," but traditional Lutheran services cannot meaningfully engage these people.

"Sunday morning they sing hymns only traditional Christians know. They use religious language that only Christians can understand. Sermons are preached that become dull, boring, and uninteresting to the lost because they don't have any 'assumed prior knowledge.' Churchy rites and rituals are practiced. Sure, much of our traditional heritage has meaning and value—but only to those who understand by having been indoctrinated to it."[11]

Kallestad further observed that the culture's pervasive entertainment media so conditions people today that, to compete for and sustain people's attention, what the church does on Sunday morning has to be stimulating, fast paced, interesting, engaging, and even "fun." Worship can be, and should be, "entertaining." He assured his readers that "the changeless message remains the same," that the church only needs to consider "stylistic changes, not substance change."

Church leaders should be aware of the sequence of responses the article stimulated, in letters to the editor.

Phase One: Immediately, in nearly 100 letters, the article attracted unprecedented "flak"! One letter suggested that the Community Church of Joy was guilty of "the old bait-and-switch crookedness used by some businesses." Another pleaded, "Give me Christ crucified, risen, and proclaimed, not P. T. Barnum." Another warned the churches against "caving in to sitcom religiosity." Still another announced that " 'entertainment evangelism' is a contradiction in terms," and that "worship that is entertainment lacks integrity with the audience that gathers."

Kallestad's detractors all shared two things. First, they assumed that anything that entertains is only "Show Biz" entertainment—of the worst kind, and could not possibly be a useful or faithful way to communicate anything worthwhile, much less the gospel. Second, the detractors totally ignored Kallestad's foundational concern for "penetrating . . . the culture." Most of the detractors had no informed understanding of what anthropologists and missiologists mean by "culture," and had not thought about the matter. Those who had thought about it saw Western culture, particularly the culture of entertainment, as only a corrupting evil to be avoided. One writer claimed, "When we try to adapt Christianity to the entertainment medium, we lose Christianity to the entertainment medium."

Phase Two: In the ensuing weeks, however, the editor tells us that "scores of letter-writers came to Kallestad's defense." One writer affirmed Kallestad for being "bold enough to try something new. I wonder where the Lutheran confessing movement would be today if Martin Luther had not been as bold!" A Winter attendee at the Community Church of Joy affirmed the church and reported that he had never witnessed there the "circus" depicted by the stereotypers. Another observed that the critics misperceived entertainment as something that merely "tickles the fancy," missing the deeper facts that entertainment, with the capacity to stimulate insight and shape values, is "transformative." Doug James, of Billings, Montana wrote:

> While the First Church of Frigidaire objects to "entertainment evangelism," does it have a better idea? The challenge we face is to make worship more inclusive by making it meaningful for more people. Entertainment evangelism, while not a total answer, suggests an interesting alternative to the present state of stagnation.

Even Kallestad's supporters, however, lacked the kind of education or experience to take cultural dynamics as seriously as leaders of the apostolic movement believe is necessary.

More recently, United Methodism's periodical for clergy—*Circuit Rider*—devoted a theme issue to "Worship: Choices, Conflict, Change."[12] Overall, the articles reveal how little church leadership's insight about culture has advanced in half a decade. The lead article, "Our Liturgical Dilemma," by a seminary professor of theology and worship, serves as a case in point.[13]

The writer is asking whether worship should be "contemporary" or not. (It occurred to me that all worship services are "contemporary." The problem is that most of them are "contemporary" to another culture or generation than our own!)

The writer asserts that a liturgy for believers is "more specifically Christian" than one "aimed explicitly at seekers." (I confess that this had not occurred to me until I read "Our Liturgical Dilemma," and I wondered what it meant. Is the English of Queen Elizabeth I that is featured in much traditional worship "more specifically Christian" than, say, the current American English of Dan Rather? Is the bar music for which Luther and Charles Wesley wrote lyrics "more Christian" than the new music promoted by the Integrity Hosanna company? Is the stewardship preaching we hear in traditional services each year before the pledge drive "more Christian" than the "Christianity 101" preaching featured in seeker services?)

More specifically, the writer defines the issue by three questions often raised at the popular level.

1. "How can we 'liven up' our Sunday morning worship?" The writer suggests that the solution is "an encounter with the Holy One of all creation," which can be achieved through traditional worship. (Maybe, but in Missiology we observe that most people who experience an encounter with God experience it through their cultural forms rather than through alien forms, and the few people meeting God through "traditional" forms have first been reinculturated into the Christian subculture that the forms represent.)

2. "How can worship meet all the people's needs more effectively?" The writer responds by painting pre-Christian visitors into the "consumerist culture," and by suggesting that what they want is not the same thing they need. Furthermore, he declares, the church that tries to meet needs through being "relevant" can become "captive to what is merely current" and be led into "cultural captivities of various sorts: psychological, ideological, and socioeconomic." (Maybe, but some of us in Missiology perceive that the mainline American church is already in cultural captivity to its tradition's past or to eighteenth- and nineteenth-century Europe, or to its intellectuals who, in turn, are captives of Enlightenment ideology.)

3. "How can Christian worship 'target' the unchurched?" The writer responds by advising churches not to do that, because that reduces worship to "a pragmatic tool for evangelism." We should, instead, usher seekers into "faith-sharing groups, work projects, common ministries, and study for inquirers." (The writer neglects to tell us why funneling seekers into work projects and common ministries does not reduce those to mere pragmatic tools of evangelism. He does not tell us what to do on Sunday morning with pre-Christians who continue to show up—using the worship service as a shop window to see if there is anything in the Christian store for them.)

76

Besides, the experiences of the people in apostolic churches are contrary to what the writer states. When evangelism is one objective in contemporary worship, believers are reinforced in their understanding and affirmation of the gospel. Believers have many of the same needs that seekers have, so they typically respond to relevant preaching that interfaces the wisdom of scripture with their anxiety, or depression, or dead-end job, or struggling marriage. Furthermore, believers often encounter Christ afresh through the people in their midst who are meeting him for the first time.

To his credit, the writer pleads for regaining "the inner connection between liturgy and life," and for achieving "relevance to the tensions and human needs of our present age." He does not, however, make the connection we know to make in every other field of mission but our own: We connect worship to life and to people's tensions and needs by employing the forms of their culture. Our ethnic minority church leaders more often perceive this need than culture-blind Anglos. In the same issue of *Circuit Rider*, Bishop Joel Martinez observes that "unless people see themselves in the liturgy, they are not going to stay."

We have considered a case for culturally relevant Christianity. We have sketched the several forms of "Contemporary" or "Seeker" services, with some attention to the censure often directed at these services. Specific instruction for developing a Seeker Service is beyond the scope of this book; I recommend *A Community of Joy: How to Create Contemporary Worship* by Timothy Wright (Nashville: Abingdon Press, 1994) for church leaders desiring to implement this vision. Wright is the mind behind the contemporary seeker services at The Community Church of Joy.

Permit me this word of perspective. Contemporary, culturally appropriate worship does not by itself evangelize, and may not even attract many visitors. As we will emphasize in the last chapter, our people are the agents of evangelism. Our two purposes for offering indigenous celebrative worship are: (1) To provide a celebration to which pre-Christians can relate and find meaning, and (2) To remove "the cringe factor" by providing a service our people would love to invite their friends to, rather than a service they would dread inviting their friends to.

Extending the Vision of the Jerusalem Council

Today, church leaders sometimes discover God giving them a passion to reach an American counterculture, rather than merely another subculture. Recently, in the United Methodist Church of Moore, Oklahoma (a part of metropolitan Oklahoma City), a young man in his late twenties named Bill experienced a deeper gift of faith and began serving as a counselor in the youth ministry. He launched efforts to revitalize the Men's Fellowship, and he began reaching out to undiscipled young men. He has had two experiences that illustrate, negatively and positively, Christianity's options on the culture challenge.

First, Bill observed that most of Moore, Oklahoma's young men like to gather in the fall to watch Monday Night Football on television, and the only places providing that setting were bars. He wondered if the Men's Fellowship could bring in a large screen TV into the church's fellowship hall on Monday nights and host unchurched men. He asked an acquaintance with long hair, a left earring, and a motorcycle if guys would be interested in watching Monday Night Football at the United Methodist Church. The fellow replied, "I would like to, and I could bring other guys." When Bill proposed this Monday evening agenda to the Men's Fellowship president, he heard this reply: "Sure, we could meet on Monday nights, but we like dominos more than football; invite them to come and play *our* game."

Even with this revised agenda, Bill's friend visited the Men's Fellowship. His friend liked the men, most of whom were older, and was attracted by what he understood of Christianity's message. But he felt uncomfortable, saying to Bill, "Look, with my long hair and earring, I'm out of place here. Christianity is not for people like me. After tonight, I'm out of here." Bill found himself saying, "If I get my ear pierced, will you come back?" His friend was moved, and said, "If you care enough about me to do that, sure, I will come back, and I will bring my friends!"

Some Christian leaders are now starting new congregations, and even movements, especially targeting people who aren't at all like most "church people." Several years ago, a forty-year-old pastor named Bob Beeman experienced a vision for reaching rebellious, drug abusing, "Baby Buster" teenagers and young adults—some of them suicidal, many of them influenced by occult practices, most of them loving heavy metal music. Beeman launched, from the Los Angeles area, "Sanctuary"—a new network of churches now found in many West Coast cities. Though Beeman is a conventional middle-class son of a parsonage family and a lover of the Glenn Miller big-band music from the 1930s and 40s, he bit the aesthetic bullet. Beeman now preaches in a black shirt, blue jeans, and snakeskin boots; his services feature the heavy metal band "Barren Cross." Sanctuary's growing ministries include a toll-free 800 phone line, Boot Camp Bible Studies for new believers, and especially "RAD Studies" (RAD standing for Radical Active Discipleship). By communicating to Baby Busters through their culture, Sanctuary churches now reach, in each city where they have a ministry, hundreds of people whom no other churches would be reaching.[14]

So, some pioneering Christians and churches are demonstrating the Christian movement's way forward in our secular mission field by *extending* the decision of the Jerusalem Council. They have discovered that we do not usually reach people by requiring them to become like us culturally, though a few will become "kosher" church people to become Christians. We will reach many more people when some of us are willing to "become kosher" and adopt enough of their culture to identify with them, and communicate through their culture's forms, creating whatever new units and ministries that are necessary, and thereby helping them discover the gospel as good news for people like them.

A Challenge to the Church from . . . Hollywood

Even Hollywood seems to be challenging the Church to forsake its cultural captivity, to identify with unchurched people and their struggles and their community, and to offer culturally indigenous worship and music that will actually *attract* unchurched secular people.

Perhaps you saw the movie *Sister Act*, staring Whoopi Goldberg and Maggie Smith. As the movie opens, Whoopi Goldberg is a nightclub performer in Las Vegas who witnesses a murder. The police hide her out in a Roman Catholic convent where she is to live, for the time being, as a nun. She and the other nuns attend the local parish church that is adjacent to the convent, where a nun's choir sings badly before an almost empty church, where the priest announces, "We are a small congregation this morning. Too many mornings. Something has gone terribly wrong. Where is faith? Where is celebration? Where is everyone?"

Whoopi Goldberg accepts the challenge to lead the choir and reform the music. As the choir of nuns now sings "Hail, Holy Queen" under her direction, the harmony, the style, the energy, and the spontaneous life in their music are so different that people in the street hear the music and are attracted to the church. Though Maggie Smith, the convent's Mother Superior, resists the new style, the priest and Whoopi Goldberg maneuver the freedom for the nuns to continue the new music style, and also to leave the convent daily in conversation and service with the people of a rather dangerous community outside. They develop a day care center, and a food kitchen for homeless people, and they converse, laugh, and pray with the people in the community. Their reputation spreads and the church grows. In the movie's final scene the pope has come to the church that is now full, to observe this wonder.

The movie's most important moment occurs after the first service in which Whoopi Goldberg leads the choir. The exchange between Whoopi,

Maggie, and the priest, in the choir room after the service, shows Maggie Smith beginning to get in touch with the discovery that could transform thousands of congregations:

Maggie Smith to Whoopi Goldberg: "Boogie Woogie on the piano? What were you thinking?"
Whoopi Goldberg: "I was thinking more like Vegas; you know, get some butts in the seats."
Maggie Smith: "And what next? Popcorn? Curtain calls? This is not a theater or a casino!"
Whoopi Goldberg: "Yeah, but that's the problem see. People like going to theaters, and they like going to casinos. But they don't like coming to church. Why? Because it's a drag. But we could change all that see. We could pack this joint."
Maggie Smith: "Through blasphemy? You have corrupted the entire choir!"

The priest overhears the conversation as Maggie Smith announces that Whoopi should lead the choir no more. He enters the choir room, and engages in a redemptive bluff worthy of any Las Vegas poker dealer, saying to Maggie Smith: "Reverend Mother, I just wanted to congratulate you. I haven't enjoyed mass this much in years. What a marvelous program—innovative, inspiring—you are to be commended. I can't wait until next Sunday when the choir performs again. Did you see the people walk right in from the street? That music, that heavenly music! Reverend Mother, it called to them."

She replied: "It . . . it did?"

✛

How Small Groups Shape an Apostolic People

I had just moved, in 1968, to serve as pastor of the Sparkhill Methodist Church in the southern "inner-belt" of Birmingham, England. A generation of West Indian and Pakistani immigration had changed that part of Birmingham demographically. A core of 50 Anglos still attended Sparkhill church—making possible a mission to the West Indian immigrant population. In reaching this new population, Sparkhill church experienced more continuity with the past than one might expect. Since the West Indies people spoke "better English" than did the British, and since they loved the Wesleyan hymns even more than did the British Methodists, this provided a liturgical continuity that enabled us to reach the new population even as we retained many long-time Anglo members.

Furthermore, the West Indies Methodists had breathed new life into the old Wesleyan "class meeting" tradition. I had only read about Wesleyan class meetings. They largely died out in American Methodism while Francis Asbury was still with us, a period when the Camp Meeting appeared to be the wave of the future and replaced the class meeting as American Methodism's distinctive institution. So I had never been a member of a "class," nor had I ever attended a class meeting, or seen one.

So I anticipated the Tuesday evening when I would attend Methodism's distinctive version of the "small group." As Sparkhill church's lay leader and I walked down a block of "flats" and small homes, I observed (through a bay window) a group of people in a meeting, and asked, "Is that it?" "No," my host replied, "That is my cousin's house; an Alcoholics Anonymous group meets there Tuesday evenings." I noticed a group in the living room of the next house: "Is that it?" "No," he said, "but, depending on who you talk to, that is either the joke or the scandal of the neighborhood. You are viewing the Communist cell group that meets in that home!" The next home hosted the Methodist class meeting.

The Varied Agendas of Small Groups

I have never forgotten the lesson of that evening. "Small groups" were meeting in three adjacent homes. From the street they looked "the same." Yet they were pursuing such different agendas that about the only thing they had in common was that they were pursuing their respective agendas through the small group context. Each group was defined much more by its agenda than by its context. Since that night, I have seldom been seduced by the usual assumption that all small groups are more or less "the same." That assumption scripts many church leaders to respond to any proposal to start small groups with the words "We tried that once. It didn't work here."

Perhaps an analogy will highlight my point. Few people assume that, for example, football, soccer, rugby, baseball, and cricket are the same sport. Someone could say that since each sport involves two teams, in uniforms, contesting for a ball, in a stadium, in front of partisan fans, then they must be more or less the same sport. Such a conclusion would not be impossible. (Some people suggest, from a similar way of reasoning, that all religions are the same!) However, I have never heard anyone say these several sports are the same. To be sure, some are more alike than others, as football is more like soccer than like cricket, but to say that football is the same as soccer would ignore the thousand or more features that make each sport sui generis. So, to say that "we tried groups here" makes no more sense than to say "we tried sports here."

I am not "splitting hairs" in elaborating this point. There are compelling reasons for churches to take another look at "small groups," specifically at several of the many agendas that are best pursued (or only pursued) in the small group. The apostolic congregations all feature small groups prominently. Some of them define themselves as churches of small groups; small groups are even more important in their identity as a church than the large worship service. Why? They have discovered a transformative power in the small group revolution that many other churches still need to discover.

Biblical Precedents for Small Groups

One reason for considering small groups is biblical. The early church experienced two structures as necessary and normative for the Messianic movement. They met as cells (or small groups) in "house churches"; and the Christians of a city also met together in a common celebration or congregation (except for periods when persecution prohibited public celebrations and drove the movement underground, meeting in homes only).

This twofold structure is reflected in the Acts of the Apostles and elsewhere in the New Testament. Jesus first modeled this pattern by gathering and mentoring the twelve disciples as a group, as well as worshiping in the synagogue and speaking to the crowds. Acts 2 suggests that the earliest Christian movement, following Peter's sermon at Pentecost, organized the 3,000 people who responded into cells that met in homes, while the entire movement in Jerusalem also gathered at the Temple (likely the court area adjacent to the Temple). After they experienced a period of public preaching, compassionate ministries, signs and wonders, and continued growth (Acts 2:47, 4:4, 5:14), they still met in the temple courts and in homes (Acts 5:42). The potent passage in Acts 2:42-47 tells us that these early Christians:

- studied the apostles' teachings,
- experienced the fellowship,
- broke bread together,
- prayed together,
- pooled resources to meet one another's needs,
- enjoyed one another's company,
- praised God,
- built rapport with the wider population in Jerusalem, and
- engaged in outreach that led to further growth.

The passage is not explicit about which experiences were typical of the cell, and which of the larger gathering, though we can infer. As the movement expanded far beyond Jerusalem, the twofold structure accompanied it. Luke tells us that Paul and Silas, after their liberation from the jail in Macedonia, visited the church that met in Lydia's home (Acts 16:40). In Ephesus, Paul taught the Christians in their large public gatherings as well as "from house to house" (Acts 20:20).[1] Paul refers, in two of his letters, to the house church in Corinth that met in the home of Prisca and Aquila (see Romans 16:5 and 1 Corinthians 16:19). Elsewhere, he refers to the church meeting in the home of Nympha in Laodicea (Colossians 4:15). Furthermore, the movement not only seems to have planted small house churches wherever it spread, it also seems to have intentionally multiplied house churches in each city it reached.[2] The small group was an essential structure for early Christianity.[3]

Reformation Precedents for Small Groups

John Wesley predicated the expansion of one of the "apostolic" branches of the Protestant Reformation substantially upon the small groups he called "classes." Wesley wanted his movement to recover the full message, vision, power, and contagion of "the Primitive Church." He was a student of primitive Christianity as reflected in the New Testament, particularly the Pastoral Epistles. He was also an astute observer of the eighteenth-century Church of England—which was largely devoid of apostolic vision, power, and contagion, and therefore "a fallen church." I have discussed, elsewhere, Wesley's understanding of what took place in the small groups of early Christianity and their connection with the vision, power, and contagion that needed to be recovered.

> Wesley . . . observed that certain normative behaviors were characteristic of life in the primitive church. They met together "to stir up one another to love and good works . . . encouraging one another" (Hebrews 10:24-25). They seemed to have taught, admonished, exhorted, and prayed for one another. They rejoiced with those who rejoiced, and wept with those who wept (Romans 12:15). Their behaviors toward one another ranged from telling one's sins to one another (Matthew 18:15-18), to building one another up (1 Thessalonians 5:11). And Wesley believed the earliest churches followed the script of James 5:16: "Confess your sins to one another, and pray for one another, that you may be healed." With regret, Wesley did not see such behavior in his Anglican Church. One of the causes of this, he believed, was the lack of small groups.
>
> Wesley ventured a revolutionary hypothesis: that *the occurrence of the first phenomenon* (faith, hope, power, and so on) *depends on the second.* That is, as you gather Christians and seekers together to confess their sins, encourage one another, rejoice together, and so forth, the life, love, faith, hope, and power of the Apostolic church emerges. He sensed that if he drew people together in cells to challenge and encourage each other to live daily as Christians, through their protracted experiences, the contagion and power of the Apostolic church would move in human history once again. And it happened![4]

Wesley was at least as much borrower as innovator, and this is especially the case in his development of ministries through small groups. He learned from his exposure to the home groups (the "ecclesiolae in ecclesia") that the Lutheran Pietist leader Philip Jacob Spener developed to fuel renewal and outreach, and Wesley learned particularly from the Moravians.[5] Wesley also learned from Anabaptist groups and from the occasional "societies" within the Church of England, so his group movement was eclectic Protestant.

Eighteenth-century British Methodism featured several types of groups. The "class" was the primary group; every Methodist belonged to a class. Indeed, the class was Methodism's main point of entry for "awakened" seekers who had not yet experienced justification and new life but who desired such experience. People, believers and seekers, first joined a class that met weekly. People who remained earnest in their pursuit of a new life, and participated faithfully in the weekly class meetings, automatically joined the local Methodist "Society" after three months.[6] A Methodist Society was composed of the sum total of classes attached to it. As one's membership in early Christianity was primarily to a house church and somewhat secondarily to the whole Church within the city, so in early Methodism one's primary membership was in the class and somewhat secondarily in the society.

Early Methodism also provided another group, the Band, for Christians who were eager to undertake the disciplines for becoming all they were created to be. Then, the Penitent Bands were provided for people who had lapsed from serious discipleship and were now seeking restoration. So, most of what early Methodism achieved in the lives of people was achieved through its network of small groups.

One of Wesley's strategies for the movement's expansion was "Start as many classes as you can." Indeed, Wesley regarded the teaching, account-ability, and nurture of the class as so essential for seekers that he advised against "awakening" a spiritual quest within people without involving people in classes. Why? Because "the devil himself desires nothing more than this, that the people of any place should be half-awakened and then left to themselves to fall asleep again." Wesley and his people learned, the hard way, that awakening religious interest in people without bringing them into group life was "only begetting children for the murderer."[7]

New Hope: A Church of Small Groups

Dale Galloway, the founding pastor of New Hope Community Church in Portland, Oregon, is a significant pioneer in small groups ministries today. New Hope has been built essentially on the principle that Carl George has named the "Metachurch" principle. New Hope is not a church with small groups, but a church of about 625 small groups, whose people also meet in the large celebration. Galloway is an advocate of this "20/20 vision."

The way to build a great church is to follow the master plan that was so effective in the early church. Meet in the house of God on Sunday to celebrate all together the resurrection power of Jesus. Then, throughout the week, meet house-to-house in small groups for heart-to-heart fellowship. This New Testament blueprint for building a successful church is in perfect step with meeting the needs of people who are lonely and isolated in this twentieth century. This plan is absolutely perfect for this generation.[8]

New Hope's leaders believe that only the Christian small group can meet the deep needs in driven, stressed, "Type A" urban personalities today. Indeed, small groups meet the very needs reflected in the theme song of the television show *Cheers:*

> Making your way in the world today takes everything you've got.
> Taking a break from all your worries sure would help a lot.
> Wouldn't you like to get away?
> Sometimes you want to go where everybody knows your name,
> and they're always glad you came.
> You want to be where you can see our troubles are all the same.
> You want to go where people know people are all the same.
> You want to go where everybody knows your name.

Consequently, New Hope is built today on over 600 "Tender Loving Care" (TLC) Groups composed of eight to ten families, each group averaging from 6 to 20 in average weekly attendance, though the ideal is 8 to 12. The TLC groups are led by "lay pastors," male or female, who also serve as the lay pastor for each person in the group. The TLC groups generally follow a prescribed study—often written by the Senior Pastor, usually a Bible study based on a book of the Bible, or a theme that is studied from multiple passages. However, the TLC groups are not primarily Bible study groups. Three things, which reflect even more the TLC group's essence, are supposed to occur in each weekly meeting:

• Sharing
• Conversational prayer
• Biblical application

So, group members share their hopes, pains, sins, struggles, and experiences with one another. They draw together spiritually through short sentence prayers in which the group converses with God. They study the Bible for the purpose of applying its revelation, promises, wisdom, and insights to their daily lives. (Participants do not do any "homework" between meetings; if homework was required or expected, then only "students" would come and the group would be a class, and not a healing fellowship.) One group may spend more time on one of these three activities than another group, but the groups are built on all three of those things taking place every time they meet.

New Hope Community Church features three types of groups, each with its own distinct agenda. (1) Nurture groups primarily focus on caring for one another—through sharing, prayer, and biblical application, though they often share in a project or ministry outside the life of the group. (2) Support groups, like New Hope's many 12 Step Groups, revolve around the needs that the group members have in common, with the focus on overcoming and healing. (3) Task groups are teams of people involved in some task or ministry—like ushers, greeters, the worship band, or adult youth sponsors, who focus primarily on a task or ministry, but who also meet regularly as a group for sharing, prayer, and biblical application. (New Hope and most other apostolic congregations believe it is very important for all the people involved in a specific ministry to meet, function, and be identified as a group. They also report that many people—especially men—who really need a group experience, but resist "joining a group," will commit to a task whose participants "also" meet as a group! Furthermore, if a church starting a group movement organizes the people already in-volved in each task or ministry into a "group," this one step gives great momentum to the church's new small groups emphasis.)

The three types of groups are different from one another in degree, and in their focus. Nevertheless, every group has an empty chair, as a symbol of the group's mission to reach at least one new person every six months; for this purpose, most New Hope groups are "open" for new group members (but not "drop-ins"), believers or seekers.[9] Each type of group experiences sharing, praying, and biblical application, and the leader's role in each group meeting is more to facilitate each person's participation than to function as an "expert." Then, in his or her lay pastor role, the leader is in contact with people between meetings—as servant, shepherd, and evan-gelist. The best of the TLC groups become families, in which the members pull for one another and build up one another in faith and self-esteem.

New Hope Community Church's TLC emphasis is much more "high expectation" or "high demand" than we find in most churches. The groups meet every week. The leader signs a one-year (renewable) contract to serve both as group leader and as lay pastor. Lay pastors with vocational and family responsibilities typically serve four to six hours per week, though some financially independent persons may lead several groups and pastor a much larger "flock." Lay pastors and assistant lay pastors must first take a weekend of training before assuming leadership of any group. Once involved as leaders, they are expected to attend a weekly leaders' meet-ing—where they submit reports from last week's meeting, study the lesson for their next group meeting, and receive further training in lay ministry and small group leadership.[10] The leaders recruit members for their groups. Each group is expected to welcome a new Christian or seeker into its ranks every six months, and is expected to sponsor new TLC groups and to identify and develop new leaders; lay pastors are recognized as "senior lay pastors" when such "fruits" are evident.

New Hope's group ministry is organized to permit infinite expansion. Each TLC group has three leaders: a lay pastor, a host or hostess, and a lay pastor trainee—who will, in time, start a new TLC group or assume leadership of the present one. The groups are organized by districts. The district pastors visit each group in their districts from time to time—to help and encourage—and the group leaders report to their district pastors. The majority of New Hope's groups are in geographic districts (50 to 60 groups per district), but in recent years New Hope has added "specialty" districts. By 1993, New Hope had organized eight specialty districts:

• Positive Singles District
• New Life Victorious District
• Children's District
• Youth District
• Young Adult District
• Women's District
• Music District
• Tasks District

The Music District is composed of groups involved in the church's music ministry. The Tasks District contains groups of people performing various services, like ushering. The New Life Victorious District features recovery groups for more than 600 people with various addictions, and so on; each group is led by a lay pastor who is recovering from that same addiction. (If all of that seems like a lot of structure for a small groups ministry, New Hope's leaders reply that traditional churches have a highly structured business side, with committees, budgets, meetings, audits, and so on. By contrast, apostolic congregations streamline the structure of their business side and they structure for ministry thoroughly enough to permit achievement and expansion.)

How do you start such small groups in your church? Galloway and New Hope Community Church have produced impressive and useful resources for other churches to study and adapt (see the appendix, Selected Resources), and New Hope also holds three Church Growth Institutes each year (on the first weekend of February, May, and October). In the Friday evening and Saturday sessions of those institutes, participants attend the actual training that New Hope gives to a new cadre of lay pastor/small group leaders. Short of a full study of their resources, Galloway offers this useful perspective: "You may not like my answer. The worst mistake a pastor can make is to divide the whole parish into parts and then assign a leader over each part thinking that suddenly he is going to have all these alive, successful home cell groups." Instead, he advises the pastor to start the process by forming one of the two or three original groups, to learn the principles of small group ministry, to teach them to others, and to develop leaders slowly. "It takes patient work over three or four years to put the groundwork in before you are ready for mass duplication."[11]

In *20/20 Vision: How to Create a Successful Church*, Galloway offers this prescription for starting a specific group:

> The first thing to do when starting a TLC group is to determine who will be the leader, assistant leader, and host or hostess.
>
> Next, determine exactly when and where the group will be meeting on a regular weekly basis. Then, set the date for the first meeting. This first meeting should be a time of fellowship and getting acquainted. Serve light refreshments. Your goal is to get people to enjoy being with each other and to challenge them to come back each week for the Tender Loving Care group that is planned.
>
> Where do people come from? Build your prospect list by writing down anyone and everyone you can think of as a prospective member. . . . In our church we have thousands of prospects who are divided on our mailing list into the zip codes. Most of those starting a new TLC group can receive almost unlimited prospects from the District Pastor, taken from the mailing list of the people who live in that zip code.
>
> However, people are not required to attend a Tender Loving Care group in their particular zip code area. The leader may invite anyone whom God has laid on his heart.
>
> Here is the three part formula that will work every time: build your prospect list—pray your prospect list—and work your prospect list.[12]

New Hope's leaders believe that the New Hope experiment has demonstrated that the "20/20" small group strategy can reach lost people, grow them into strong Christians, give people opportunities for ministry and service, fill believers with enthusiasm, and develop a new generation of Christian leaders in local churches. Like a one-a-day multivitamin, the TLC group "does it all." The strategy's relevance becomes obvious when we are confronted with associate pastor David Durey's arresting question: "If God dumped 100 converts on your doorstep today, how would you handle them? What would be the best system to disciple them and see them grow?" Small lay-led groups provide the only adequate answer.

The management of an expanding small groups system is hard work, but not nearly so hard as the staff trying to shepherd 6,000 people by themselves! Galloway believes that, in principle, the proliferation of lay-led small groups can provide for "unlimited growth." That may sound extravagant, but the Yoido Central Full Gospel Church of Seoul, Korea has been following a similar strategy for many years. The last I heard, their membership had passed 800,000! Most of their members are first-generation Christians, who were first reached, and are now experiencing growth, through one or another of the church's 60,000 lay-led home cell groups!

Saddleback: A Church with Small Groups

Saddleback Valley Community Church provides an interesting contrast to New Hope in its small groups ministry. Saddleback defines itself as a "purpose driven" church and has stopped short of defining itself as a church of small groups. Saddleback is a church with small groups, however, and small groups play an indispensable role in their total strategy as a church and their development of people. See, for example, the role played by small groups in "The Saddleback Strategy" using Rick Warren's "Saddleback" acronym:

- Seeker Sensitive Services
- Affinity Groups
- Driven by Purpose
- Defined Target
- Life Development Process
- Every Member a Minister
- Behavioral Preaching
- Authentic Leadership
- Climate of Acceptance
- Keep the Structure Simple

Saddleback Church also features small groups very early in their approach to developing disciples, as seen in the church's well-known "Baseball Diamond" analogy for developing strong Christians. Their four objectives (or "bases") for people are Knowing Christ, Growing in Christ, Serving Christ, and Sharing Christ. These four objectives are related to four commitments they envision for people—commitments to Membership, Maturity, Ministry, and Mission. More specifically, the life development process suggested by these categories is built around four 4-hour seminars that Saddleback labels 101, 201, 301, and 401! The second seminar, 201, that invites people to commit to their own Maturity, specifically invites people to join a small group, as well as adopt a daily devotional discipline and a regular stewardship discipline.

Small groups are important to Saddleback's approach to church growth: they believe that as a church grows larger it must also grow "smaller"—by starting small groups that support church growth and personal growth and help people feel like they "belong." Saddleback's leaders believe, as do New Hope's, that the twofold small group/large celebration structure is modeled in the New Testament and is necessary for the existence of healthy, powerful, and contagious Christianity.

Associate pastor Tom Holladay adds a practical reason for having small groups be lay led, and for having them meet in homes: Growing churches cannot afford to add staff or build facilities fast enough to reach the world or to support the growth that is already happening! Using homes and gifted laity is the better way to employ the physical and human resources already entrusted to us. The home groups strategy is infinitely expandable, and the setting "promotes fellowship and relationship building better than metal chairs in a Sunday school room." Within Saddleback's small groups emphasis, some 200 groups meet in a typical week, involving 2,600 people— over one-half of Saddleback's 4,600 membership.

Saddleback features four types of groups, based on the specific purposes they serve. About 70 percent to 75 percent of their groups are Community groups that meet in homes and focus on fellowship, sharing, and ministry to one another. The church also offers Care groups—for people needing recovery from an addiction or support through grief or some other experience. The church offers Growth groups—for people needing rootage in scripture or doctrine, or accountability in discipleship. Saddleback also offers Mission Groups that engage in outreach to people in the wider community.

Saddleback especially believes in encouraging groups to organize around "affinities" and they give "affinity groups" a lot of freedom in what they study, and do. The reason for the "affinity" and "freedom" themes relates to the group's "energy." Saddleback's leaders have learned that if you do not group people by affinity (based on a common culture, concern, crisis, or commitment), then the leader has to provide most of the glue that holds the group together! Moreover, Tom Holladay reports that "if you put a leash on your small groups, they will pull you around! You have to be willing to let go."

Saddleback's emphases upon groups defining their own agenda and choosing their own curriculum illustrates how their program varies with a (still) higher expectation church like New Hope—most of whose groups follow a prescribed curriculum most of the time. There are several other ways in which these two small groups ministries contrast. New Hope contracts with its group leaders to serve also as lay pastors. Saddleback followed that model for several years, but backed off. Like New Hope (and many other churches), Saddleback discovered that recruiting people to join groups is (much) easier than recruiting people to lead groups; their groups ministry has grown only as fast and as large as the number of gifted, trained, and willing group leaders has permitted. Saddleback additionally discovered that many people gifted for group leadership resist being identified as, or expected to function as, a pastor. So Saddleback split those roles; the church still has (many) lay pastors, but that role is no longer hyphenated to the role of group leader.

New Hope's groups meet weekly. Some of Saddleback's groups (and most groups in many other churches) meet every other week, though most of their groups meet weekly, and Recovery Groups need to meet every week.

Within several months of their initial formation, most of Saddleback's groups become more or less closed groups—with a life expectancy of about two years. Most of New Hope's groups are open groups, and they are expected to reach someone new every six months; their groups have a longer life expectancy—perhaps because the periodic new members reconstitute the group to some degree.

The two churches vary in their ongoing expectations of group leaders. New Hope expects group leaders to file a report weekly; Saddleback expects only a monthly report of the group's name and its average attendance for the month. New Hope expects attendance at a weekly training meeting for all group leaders; Saddleback requires that group leaders meet monthly with their district lay pastor, and quarterly for large-scale training.

The place of Saddleback's small groups ministries within their total growth strategy can be expressed in terms of three "doors." The church's "front door" is its four Seeker Sensitive worship services each weekend; most people enter the church's life through that port of entry. The small groups function as a "side door" through which some people enter the church's life, particularly the recovery groups. The small groups perform a very important role in relation to the church's "back door." The small groups close the back door for people who become involved in a group; effectively "assimilated" and included people do not look for the back door.

Willow Creek: A Church with Groups Goes "Metachurch"

Willow Creek Community Church began with a deep appreciation of the role of small groups, particularly in the life of a new convert needing discipling. Willow Creek has always included small groups in their well-known "Seven Step Strategy":

1. A Christian (Gary) builds a friendship with "Unchurched Harry," and prays for an opening to share some Good News.
2. Gary responds to the opening, shares some Good News and begins evangelical conversations with Harry.
3. Gary takes Harry to a weekend "Seekers Service," to which Harry returns for months.
4. When Harry believes and wants to follow Christ, he joins and attends the midweek New Community.
(In joining, Harry also agrees to steps 5, 6, and 7.)
5. Harry joins, and meets with, a small group for the first two years of his new life.
6. Harry discovers his spiritual gifts and passions and becomes involved in a ministry.
7. Harry builds a friendship with "Unchurched Larry" and the cycle is repeated.[13]

So Willow Creek considered small groups to be necessary for the first two years of a convert's new life, and optional (though very desirable) for other Christians. By the early 1990s however, the church had experienced such remarkable growth that the church was forced to include everyone in groups—because, even with a staff of 300, there was no other way to provide ongoing care and nurture for all the members and constituents! Willow Creek's *Church Leaders Handbook* explains:

> As Willow Creek continued to grow, staff members were increasingly unable to adequately care for those in their ministries and in the church at large, and were faced with the prospect of either hiring more staff or letting needs go unmet. The former was declared impractical, the latter unthinkable. What was needed was a decentralized system that released the laity to minister within adequate spans of care. The small group structure, based on Jethro's advice to Moses in Exodus 18 and the meta-church theories advanced by Carl George and Greg Ogden, answered that need by providing a strategy through which everyone is cared for, and no one cares for more than ten.[14]

Willow Creek's leaders discovered that the change from a church with small groups to a church of small groups rearranges virtually every ball on the billiard table. The most strategic people in the whole system now are not the paid staff, but the small group leaders. The staff's role changed from primarily doing ministry to primarily facilitating the ministries of the laity. Organizationally, the church became much more decentralized, and, since the whole church is now a church of groups, the old department of small groups closed shop. Willow Creek organized their already extensive cadre of laity doing ministries into groups doing ministries, and they emphasized the training of persons gifted to be group leaders. The result, after three years, is about 8,000 people involved in about 1,100 groups.

Willow Creek's leaders believe, with those of other apostolic congregations, that the cell and the celebration are the two "micro" and "macro" structures modeled and implicitly mandated in the Acts of the Apostles. They now have the experience-based conviction that small groups provide "the optimal environment for the life-change Jesus Christ intends for every believer."[15] They believe that every believer must be connected to other believers, so this mandates the existing groups to expand and multiply. Therefore every group features the symbolic "empty chair" and every group has a stake in the birthing of new groups. Willow Creek defines what its groups do together in terms of four verbs: Love, Learn, Decide, Do.[16]

Four Components of Small Group Life

- Love: Group members caring for one another, and sharing in each other's lives through accountability, prayer, and intentional acts of service to one another.
- Learn: Group members experiencing a growing knowledge of God and themselves.
- Decide: Group members making decisions about curriculum, activities, and schedule.
- Do: Group members participating in an activity, or serving in a task together.

The group leader's role is to facilitate the meeting around those four components, and to shepherd the members between meetings, as well as to develop new leaders and multiply the ministry. The group leader is also God's front line care-giver during a crisis for a group member, with group members and church staff playing appropriate supporting roles during the crisis.

Willow Creek's small groups ministries represent the church's desire to be a biblical community, and to help people become totally devoted followers of Jesus Christ. All of Willow Creek's groups share the church's vision, mission, and core values; all of the groups engage in loving, learning, deciding, and doing; all of the groups want to connect people to God, each other, and the church.

All of Willow Creek's groups exist in a structure that involves a Small Group Leader (leader of 10), an Apprentice (coleader of 10), a Coach (leader of 50), and a Division Leader (leader of 500). All of those leaders are involved in the "Leadership Community" that meets monthly for vision-ing, training, and the huddling of group leaders and apprentices with their coaches.

Like New Hope and Saddleback, Willow Creek features several types of groups. The church's handbook for small-group leaders explains:

> To accommodate the many needs and levels of maturity of attenders of Willow Creek, a variety of small groups have been developed. Groups typically form around areas of affinity such as marital status, age, ministry, task, personal need, life stage, etc. Virtually every group could be placed in one of the five major categories below. Though we recognize the autonomy and distinctiveness of each individual small group, most groups can be characterized as one of the five listed below.
>
> *Disciple Making Groups*, for believers, follow the Willow Creek "Walking With God" resources now published by Zondervan. These groups intentionally root believers in scripture, Christian understanding, and spiritual disciplines. They meet twice monthly for 18 to 24 months.
>
> *Community Groups*, for believers and nonbelievers, exist to help their members become like Christ, to love one another, to invite new people to fill the open chair, and to birth new groups. They meet twice monthly and are expected to birth a new group after 24 to 36 meetings.
>
> *Service Groups*, for believers and nonbelievers, exist to perform and achieve a ministry or task, and also to reach new people and grow Christians. The meet weekly. The rate at which they grow and reproduce depends on the ministry.
>
> *Support Groups*, for believers and nonbelievers, meet to support group mem-bers as they work through grief, or separation, or an addiction, or some other personal difficulty. These meet weekly; their duration varies with the group's agenda and the members' needs.
>
> *Seeker Groups*, predominantly for nonbelievers, are Willow Creek's most recent major experiment in group life. Their purpose is to lead seekers to Christ and to disciple new converts. Their agenda and curriculum are shaped around the questions of the group's members. They meet every other week, and they appear (at this early stage in their development) to meet for about a year.[17]

Willow Creek's rationale for the growth and multiplication of small groups is especially cogent:

> A small group does not ultimately exist for itself. Christ-like people resist the urge to be selfish—they desire to include other unconnected people in such a way that they too may experience group life. Small groups therefore must have a viable strategy for growth and reproduction so that someday everyone

who gathers as a part of the local church is included in some kind of identifiable relational connection. . . .

Success in leadership of a small group is ultimately seen in the viability of daughter groups. The goal is not just to start a new group, but to birth a group that is healthy and creates life-change. The new group can only be considered viable if it eventually births a new group itself. In this model, a "Senior Leader" is someone who's birthed at least three groups, which in turn have birthed new groups—in other words, a leader with at least three small group "grandchildren."[18]

Small Groups for Seekers

Many apostolic congregations now include pre-Christian people in their small group life. In addition to the "empty chair" that many churches challenge their believers' groups to fill every six months, several approaches to groups essentially for pre-Christian seekers are impressive in their rationale and their results.

Saddleback Valley: Lighthouse Bible Study

When Saddleback's leaders searched for an appropriate small group strategy for engaging seekers, they found that an approach pioneered by Navigators was suitable to their seeker population. Saddleback involves over 150 pre-Christian people per year in the Lighthouse Bible Study, which has a seeker orientation and is based on the Gospel of John. In weekend services that draw a lot of seekers (such as Easter), Rick Warren invites interested people to join a Lighthouse Bible Study, with three qualifications for joining a group:

1. You are not a Christian.
2. You have some serious doubts about the Bible.
3. You are intellectually open and honest enough to discuss it with other people.

From last Easter's services, 50 people enrolled in Lighthouse Bible Studies.

The Lighthouse Bible Studies are usually held in homes or offices, expressing Navigators' interest in the Christian movement penetrating, and establishing many beachheads in, the secular community. The groups are led by lay people with the spiritual gift for evangelism, after training by Navigators. Associate pastor Tom Holladay reports that Lighthouse studies have an impressive record for "cultivating the hard ground." The key resource for group leaders is *Your Home a Lighthouse*.[19] Bob and Betty Jacks have pioneered and refined the approach in New England for two decades, and Navigators reports its very widespread usefulness.

Saddleback's Lighthouse Study brochure describes the experience as "A study for those with doubts about Christianity and for those who want to see what the Bible has to say." The brochure invites people to "begin an exciting journey through the book of John. Long regarded as one of the key passages of scripture regarding God, the study helps you understand questions such as Who is God? What is He like? And, how is He relevant to my life?" Each session schedules time for people to raise other questions.

The Lighthouse studies are designed to bridge the chasm between Christians and their secular neighbors. The Lighthouse training for leaders emphasizes two objectives of the Bible studies:

1. To communicate the love of God, so that others will be drawn to Christ as Lord and Savior.
2. Help new Christians grow spiritually so that they can better communicate the love of God to others.

While the training materials are conventional in what they tell leaders to do ("Make people comfortable," "Provide a common translation for every participant," "Be sensitive to timid or turned off people," and so on), some of the prescribed "don'ts" are notable:

DON'T

- Pray at the Bible Study.
- Play religious music.
- Talk about religion or your church.
- Knock religious groups, or even discuss them.
- Have people read.
- Call on people by name for comments.
- Clique with friends.
- Talk to others in a whisper.

The leader should remind the group, beginning each session, that "our primary objective is to learn more about God, what He is like, and how He can play a role in our lives." The leader distributes a modern translation to each person, reads it aloud, and then helps the participants process the passage with questions like the following:

1. What significance does this have for us today?
2. What does this mean to you?
3. How does (or will) this affect your life?

4. What do you think this passage means?

5. What can we learn from this passage about God, Christ, ourselves, our responsibility, our relationship to others, and so on?

6. Can anybody relate to this?

7. Is there anything you do not understand about the passage?

The Lighthouse training mandates the leader to spend time with each participant socially (in addition to the scheduled Bible study meetings), to understand and love each person in the group, and to make his or her home or office a place where people can meet Christ. Lighthouse training materials express the strategy's vision in the statement of Lord George McLeod, founder of the Iona Community in Scotland:

Lift High the Cross
George McLeod

I simply argue that the Cross should be raised at the center of the marketplace as well as on the steeple of the church. I am recovering the claim that Jesus was not crucified in a cathedral between two candles; but on a cross between two thieves; on the towns' garbage heap; at a crossroad, so cosmopolitan they had to write his title in Hebrew and Latin and Greek . . . at the kind of place where cynics talk smut, and thieves curse, and soldiers gamble. Because that is where He died. And that is what He died about. That is where church-men ought to be and what church-men ought to be about.[20]

Willow Creek: Seeker Small Groups

For years, Willow Creek's leaders stressed the need and right for all seekers to remain anonymous; "Unchurched Harry" and "Unchurched Mary" were simply encouraged to attend the weekend seeker services, remaining anonymous and working through the Christian Possibility at their own pace, in their own way. In recent years however, Willow Creek perceived a shift in a large minority of their target population; a fair number of seekers now value interaction and "talking it through" more than they value or need anonymity.

So, Willow Creek has launched Seeker Groups—with the leadership of new staffer Gary Poole, who had pioneered seeker groups with Intervarsity while a student at Indiana University. Two years into this experiment, Willow Creek has 25 to 50 Seeker Groups meeting in a given season; about half meet at the church, the others in homes. From the fruits of the seeker groups, Willow Creek now has a half-dozen New Believer groups meeting.

The groups are designed to provide a positive experience for six to ten people who are at various stages of investigating Christianity. The more specific objective is to remove obstacles in the pre-Christian's spiritual journey and, when they become receptive, to provide opportunities to receive Christ and begin following him. Gary Poole tells us, in his seminar on Seeker Small Groups, that many seekers need to be:

• Accepted as they are, and not judged
• Free to identify and investigate the faith, primarily with other seekers
• Listened to and understood
• Drawn out patiently

The leader of a Seeker Small Group needs to be an open, honest, vulnerable role model for the seekers in his or her group. The leader cares and prays for them, serves as a role model, and interacts individually with seekers before, after, and in between meetings. Poole reports that seekers "don't often cross the line into faith until they get one to one attention from the leader." When group members do receive Christ "as Forgiver and Leader," the facilitator invites these new believers to share their story with the group.

Willow Creek recruits people for new seeker groups in several ways. They announce the opportunity at weekend seekers services, and ten to fifteen persons per week register their interest on a tear-off card in the bulletin. The church invites inquirers to a Hospitality Room to ask questions after each weekend service; some of those people join a seeker group. When Willow Creek offers its "Christianity 101" class, candidates for seeker groups emerge from that experience. Also, as Willow Creek's people are befriending pre-Christian people, they often refer them to a seeker group. All invitations to explore the faith through a group are handled with care and without pressure. Often, the inviter says, "Come one time, check it out." They do ask for a yes or no response to this invitation to visit a group.

The first meeting of a small group for seekers is crucial; it defines the agenda, sets the tone, and influences whether some seekers will even return. Gary Poole advises beginning the meeting with introductions, facilitated by "icebreaker" questions like "Where do you live?" "Where do you work?" and "How long have you been coming to Willow Creek?" The leader might then facilitate a somewhat deeper involvement with a question like, "What is your favorite movie you have ever seen, and why?" or, "Who is your number one advisor in life, and why?" (Poole also recommends beginning every meeting with "icebreakers.") By the fourth meeting, Poole believes it is appropriate to ask: "Describe your spiritual journey on a scale of 1 to 10; 5 is where one crosses the line into faith."

The leader asks a question about halfway through the first session that is especially important: "If you could ask Jesus Christ any question, and he would answer it, what would you ask?" The leader records all of those questions. The leader does not presume to answer them now. (Poole reports that seekers "want to be heard. They don't want quick answers shoved down their throats.") The questions become the basis for the curriculum in the following weeks. Often, the group will take up one question per week. The leader, between sessions, is challenged to find those passages in the gospels in which Jesus answers each question, or those passages in which Jesus' answer can be inferred.

In the next sessions, the leader does not simply announce Jesus' answers; the leader helps the group to discover Jesus' answer through group study of the relevant passage(s), with the group or the leader finally stating the truth as accurately and memorably as possible at the session's conclusion. Once the original questions have been addressed through scripture study, other questions will come to the surface, or the leader may bring to the surface questions for the group to explore through scripture. For example, the leader might ask: "Describe when you lost something valuable, and what it felt like, and what happened when it turned up." That then prepares the group for a study of the three parables of Luke 15, with the group discovering something about how God feels when he doesn't have a relationship with people he values. Willow Creek has found *The Serendipity Bible*, and its study guide, to be an invaluable reference tool for the seeker small group leader.

The Church on Brady: Discovery Bible Studies

The Church on Brady employs "Discovery Bible Studies" to reach pre-Christians and also to plant new urban congregations. Discovery Bible Studies were pioneered in the Philippines, India, and Kenya. Church on Brady leaders Carol Davis and Tom Wolf were impressed by the demonstrated usefulness of the approach in those three very different countries; they have found it appropriate to the culture of every ethnic population that The Church on Brady is trying to reach and serve. The studies are led by laypersons, in homes in the target community, in groups of 12 or fewer, the majority of whom are non-Christians.

Several years ago, Brady people ultimately started a congregation in Huntington Park, one of the poorest communities in greater Los Angeles, by beginning with a door-to-door survey asking six questions:

1. What do you think are some of the needs in this community?
2. What do you think are solutions to those needs or problems?
3. Do you think the Bible has anything to say about this?
4. Have you ever read the Bible yourself?
5. Would you be willing to join some neighbors in a Bible study, to discuss some solutions to problems people face?
6. (If "yes" to number 5) Would you be willing to open your home to host a group?

Every fifth home they surveyed was willing to host a Bible study! The hosts invited people in their social network to join the group. Brady lay people led a dozen Discovery studies in the Huntington Park community, and they started a daughter church. Brady's distinctive mission in the Los Angeles area basin has reached hundreds of people and started a dozen congregations using this approach. They have found that, in many communities, you can start as many Discovery Bible Studies as you have leaders to facilitate them.

The approach has the distinct advantage of not requiring that the group leader be a biblical expert; the program's six questions guide the group through the prescribed biblical passages.

The Six Questions of a Discovery Bible Study

1. What did you like?
2. What did you not like?
3. What did you not understand?
4. What did you learn about God?
5. What do we want to do in response?
6. What phrase, thought, or sentence would you take home with you?

The last three questions are the most important questions for the group's purpose, but the first three are necessary "icebreakers." Everyone has an answer to the first question. Some Christians emotionally resist the second question, but non-Christians do not. The session does not usually deal, in any thorough way, with the third question, but it appears to be psychologically necessary for some participants to verbalize what they don't understand to free them psychologically to focus on what they do understand.

While the six questions are useful in guiding groups through innumerable biblical passages, Discovery Bible Studies focus on sets of five passages for each of three different pre-Christian populations, with a follow-up five-week study for converts:

Happiness is . . .

(for educated conceptual people)

1. Psalm 1
2. Psalm 51:1-13
3. Romans 3:21-26
4. Romans 8:29-39
5. 1 Corinthians 13

Discovering Jesus

(for less educated,
oral tradition people)

1. Mark 1:21-34
2. Mark 10:13-16
3. Mark 10:17-31
4. Mark 12: 41-44
5. Luke 23: 32-43

The Power of Jesus

(for people with addictions,
abuse experience)

1. Mark 1:21-28
2. Mark 2:13-17
3. Mark 3:1-6
4. Mark 4:35-41
5. Mark 9:33-37

First Steps

(for new believers)

1. 1 Peter 1:22-25
2. Ephesians 1:11-20
3. Ephesians 4:21-32
4. Ephesians 5:1-6 (or 1-21)
5. Ephesians 6:10-18

These are some of the "nuts and bolts" that help make Discovery Bible Studies effective: A group meets in a home for about an hour, once a week, for five weeks, processing one passage each week. The study uses the same contemporary translation, such as *The Good News Bible,* and the leader distributes to each participant a photocopy of the passage for the week. The leader's hope and prayer is that, through involvement with the Scriptures and with each other, people will discover Christ and faith.

The Church on Brady has discovered certain advantages in the Discovery approach. There is much more initial receptivity to coming to a friend's home than to the church, to meeting with friends, relatives, and neighbors rather than with strangers, to meeting in their neighborhood rather than beyond it, and to joining a group rather than a church. The focus is on the Bible, not the leader. There are no "right" or "wrong" answers to the questions, and this helps non-Christians to relax. Non-Christians experience success in understanding passages from the Bible—a book they had assumed was incomprehensible. While the Evil One does not make it easy for the Christian movement anywhere, and no one can say "Jesus is Lord" except by the Holy Spirit, Carol Davis nevertheless suggests that Discovery Bible Studies are "as simple as ABC."

A. Seekers study the Bible with their *A*cquaintances.
B. The approach is *B*ible centered.
C. The Six *C*lear Questions are the heart of the Discovery movement.

Recovery and Support Groups

Alcoholics Anonymous only dates from the 1940s—when the Reverend Samuel Shoemaker, then rector of Calvary Episcopal Church in New York City, helped two converts from his ministry to draw from the Sermon on the Mount, the book of James, and their own recovery experiences to delineate the now-famous "12 Steps," and the accompanying group process, by which people could be liberated from alcohol addiction. They also formed Alcoholics Anonymous as an autonomous organization, that is, autonomous from the Church. In that period, most church people did not know how to (or want to) relate to "drunks." Alcoholics feared judgment, so were understandably reluctant to come to churches. In defense of both, no one yet had an adequate understanding of addiction.

We now know that the alcoholism with which they struggled was only the tip of an addiction iceberg. We now know that millions of people are afflicted with a range of "substance addictions"—like addictions to alcohol, nicotine, caffeine, food, heroin and other illicit drugs, valium and other prescription drugs, and so on. We also know that millions of people are afflicted with a range of "process addictions"—including gambling, sex, work, stealing, violence, power, making money, spending money, dependent relationships, and so on. We are now told that tens of millions of people in North America have an addiction or live in a codependent relationship with an addict. Shoemaker anticipated this widespread condition with his observation that "almost everyone has a Problem, is a Problem, or lives with a Problem!"

Shoemaker and the other AA founders could scarcely have imagined the extent to which some churches are now involved in recovery ministries for addicted and compulsive personalities. This ministry marks the newest dividing line between traditional congregations and apostolic congregations. Few traditional congregations feature recovery ministries (though their pastors occasionally report "We let AA use our building!"). By contrast, all of the apostolic congregations I have studied are heavily invested in recovery ministries; especially in recent years. Although 12 Step recovery ministries are a new emphasis of apostolic congregations, these ministries are consistent with the apostolic congregation's perennial emphasis upon ministry to pre-Christian people.

While apostolic congregations vary somewhat in their theological interpretation of addiction, the following themes would represent a consensus. Addiction is a deep and complex psychological and spiritual affliction. Addiction is the typical form that possessive destructive Evil has taken in our culture in this generation. People's lives get "out of control" around specific addictions or compulsions; their feelings and energy become frozen; they experience emptiness, pain, and a kind of "insanity";[21] their lives and families become "dysfunctional"; they become alienated from other people and from God. The addiction is "bigger" than the addict, so the addicts are powerless to free themselves—though addicts deny the fact (or the seriousness) of their addictions, and indulge in the illusion that they are in control. Usually, people are liberated from addiction and its effects only through the power of God as mediated through social accountability and support; the 12 Steps represent the pattern in which God's action through the social process typically works.

In their leaflet promoting their recovery ministries, Saddleback Valley Community Church uses irony to confront people who still believe they are "in control":

The 12 Steps of the Addicted and Compulsive Person
The Reviled Substandard Version

Step 1   I (not we) declared I was in complete control of my addiction/compulsion, that my life was fine and dandy—thank you very much.

Step 2   I always knew that there was no power greater than myself, but all of you needed to be restored to sanity.

Step 3   I made a decision to turn my will and my life over to the care of my addiction/compulsive behavior, because it was the only thing that understood me.

Step 4   I made a superficial and paranoid *immoral* inventory of anybody but myself.

Step 5   I admitted nothing to nobody—ever.

Step 6   I was entirely ready to have God punish you for all your defects of character.

Step 7   I humbly asked Him to bug somebody else.

Step 8   I made a list of all persons who had harmed me and became willing to take revenge upon them all.

Step 9   I took direct revenge whenever possible, especially when to do so would harm or injure them or others.

Step 10   I continued to take other people's inventory, and when they were wrong promptly told them so.

Step 11   I sought through alcohol/drugs/relationships/food/sex/ and so on to maintain unconscious contact with myself, praying only for what I wanted, when I wanted it and the power to get it.

Step 12   Having had a *spiritual death* as a result of these steps, I tried to carry this message to other addicted/compulsive people and take as many of them as I could with me.

In another leaflet, Saddleback shares the true and liberating 12 Steps, and includes scripture references that suggest the congruence of the 12 Steps with scriptural insight.

The Twelve Steps and Their Biblical Comparisons

1. We admitted we were powerless over our addictions and compulsive behaviors, that our lives had become unmanageable (Romans 7:18).

2. Came to believe that a power greater than ourselves could restore us to sanity (Philemon 2:13).

3. Made a decision to turn our will and our lives over to the care of God as we understood Him (Romans 12:1).

4. Made a searching and fearless moral inventory of ourselves (Lamentations 3:40).

5. Admitted to God, to ourselves, and to another human being, the exact nature of our wrongs (James 5:16).

6. Were entirely ready to have God remove all these defects of character (James 4:10).

7. Humbly asked Him to remove all our shortcomings (1 John 1:9).

8. Made a list of all persons we had harmed and became willing to make amends to them all (Luke 6:31).

9. Made direct amends to such people whenever possible, except when to do so would injure them or others (Matthew 5:23-24).

10. Continued to take personal inventory and when we were wrong, promptly admitted it (1 Corinthians 10:12).

11. Sought through prayer and meditation to improve our conscious contact with God as we understood Him, praying only for knowledge of His will for us and power to carry that out (Colossians 3:16).

12. Having had a spiritual experience as the result of these steps, we tried to carry this message to others, and practice these principles in all our affairs (Galatians 6:1).

In their training for addictive and compulsive people, pastors Rick Warren and John Baker demonstrate the roots of the 12 Steps in the Beatitudes, and in the broader biblical principles of conviction, conversion, surrender, confession, restitution, prayer, quiet time, witnessing, and helping one another. They declare that "our Higher Power has a name—Jesus Christ. Jesus desires a hands on, day to day, moment to moment relationship with us. He can do for us what we have never been able to do for ourselves." They admonish their people—"Don't quit before the miracle happens. With God's help, the changes that you have longed for are just *steps* away."

Saddleback Church devotes Friday evenings to "Celebrate Recovery." Between 200 and 300 people gather for (1) a Bar-B-Q supper, (2) a worship celebration—which includes an addiction-relevant lesson, and (3) smaller meetings for "sharing our experiences, strengths, and hopes with one another" in one of the following groups:

• Adult Children of Chemically Addicted
• Chemically Dependent Men
• Chemically Dependent Women
• Codependent Men's Group
• Codependent Women's Group (two groups)
• Codependent Women in a Chemically Dependent Relationship
• Eating Disorders—Women's Group
• Renewal from Sexual Addiction—Men's Group
• Veterans in Recovery
• Women in Recovery from Sexual/Physical Abuse
• S.O.S. for Teens

Saddleback's brochure, "*Celebrate Recovery:* 12 Steps With Jesus," and the church's curriculum for recovering people feature Reinhold Niebuhr's famous prayer, a version of which many people in recovery commit to memory:

Prayer for Serenity

God, grant me the serenity
to accept the things I cannot change,
the courage to change the things I can,
and the wisdom to know the difference.
Living one day at a time,
enjoying one moment at a time;
accepting hardship as a pathway to peace;
taking, as Jesus did, this sinful world as it is,
not as I would have it;
Trusting that You will make all things right
if I surrender to your will;
so that I may be reasonably happy in this life
and supremely happy with you forever in the next. **Amen.**[22]

New Hope Community Church targets addictive people and dysfunctional families even more than most apostolic congregations, and they have a longer experience than most in the range of recovery ministries. With some seasonal variation, the church involves around 600 people in recovery and support groups each week. This ministry is featured as "New Life Victorious"; a majority of the recovery and support groups meet Monday evenings. The church invites people to believe in the possibility of

Breaking the Chains
of Addictive/Compulsive Behavior
Through Education, Prayer,
and Personal Growth.

The church's literature explains that "New Life Victorious is a spiritual 12 Step program for anyone who has or wants to understand chemical dependence, addictive and compulsive behaviors that cannot be broken without support." Leaders explain that "the support groups are loving, accepting and non-threatening, led by trained recovering lay people," but "New Life groups are spiritual support groups only, not professional therapy groups or AA meetings."

The first hour on Monday evenings is devoted to a service featuring praise songs, scripture and prayer, testimonies from people reporting how their lives are changing because of healing and recovery, and an educational presentation from "a psychological, spiritual, and emotional perspective." The second hour finds people in appropriate small recovery support groups

107

which, it is announced, "are safe, confidential groups that honor your privacy." The leaders prepare people for the group experience with certain suggestions:

- Realize recovery is a process, not a one time event.
- Realize you won't get all the answers at one time.
- Realize that it takes time to establish trust.
- Realize with God's help you will be able to figure out what is best for you, and you won't need the advice of others.
- Realize that you need to come to the same group for four weeks, at least, to get connected and bonded (after four weeks you may change groups if you choose to).
- Realize that leaders are lay pastors recovering from whatever they are leading a group in recovering from.
- Realize you are not in a group to help other people, you are there for yourself.

A recent two-month term offered people 15 recovery group options for their involvement:

- Alcohol and recovery
- Women's alcohol and drug recovery
- Adult children of troubled environments[23]
- Family support for codependency[24]
- Emotional recovery[25]
- Anger control management
- Recovering teens
- Positive action for kids
- Men's prayer and share
- Women's prayer and share
- Toughlove[26]
- Adult women molested as children
- Sexual addiction recovery
- Victorious eating
- Developing healthy relationships

In other two-month terms, Monday nights offer recovery groups for people with work addiction, low self-esteem, severe stress, smoking addiction, and other addictions and compulsions.

The church also offers teaching sessions, support groups, and recovery groups Tuesday evening, Wednesday noon, Wednesday evening, and Friday evening. Some of these groups are scheduled alternatives for people with some of the same struggles as above. Others are distinct—such as groups for separation recovery, divorce recovery, grief recovery, anger management, and healthy choices.

New Hope also offers a Friday Prayer Night—described as "a safe refuge to receive prayer for the issues brought up in support groups, where people can come for part or the whole of three hours to share their pain, struggles, needs, and victories, and receive prayer for emotional, spiritual, mental, or physical needs." The church's New Life Victorious brochure features a poem (structurally reminiscent of a Kipling poem) by Amanda Bradley a brief excerpt from which reads:

> If you treasure the beauty that shows all around you
> and try to add some of your own,
>
> . . . .
>
> Then you know what it means to live life to the fullest
> and be the best "you" you can be.[27]

Dale Galloway believes that many churches in the emerging generation will be called to offer recovery and support ministries to the expanding populations who need them. Since most of these people are undiscipled, recovery and support ministries will create a second "front door" into the church. Such churches will engage in the kind of "marketing analysis" necessary to understand the people in their ministry area and what their needs and struggles are. The church will identify and develop the group leaders, who should be Christians in recovery from the specific addiction for which they will now be in ministry. (This may, necessarily, be the slowest and most deliberate part of the process, since you cannot provide a ministry for which you do not have prepared leaders.)

Our more traditional church leaders often resist the challenge to take people's needs, wants, tastes, and preferences seriously, perhaps fearing the gospel's truth will be compromised. They, therefore, take a dim view of "pandering" to people's wants, or of even giving people choices. What is the solution? Let such church leaders observe the recovery ministries in apostolic congregations, and let them interview people once broken who are being made whole. Their resistance to being "relevant" will melt like ice before the sun. Then, a focus on human needs may indeed sweep through *their* church, and they will observe God's compassion breaking through the stack of excuses for not becoming agents of God's healing for the destructive addictions all around us. Once each potential group for, say, people with alcohol addiction, work addiction, food addiction, and codependency has a leader and is scheduled, then the church can engage in extensive advertising and inviting.

In most communities the needs and opportunities for starting recovery and support groups are vast, and no institution except the church is positioned to provide the recovery ministries that millions of people need. The apostolic congregations I have studied are responding to this challenge with great entrepreneurial spirit, and the support and recovery ministries they launch instruct us on the range of the need, and on a local church's capacity to organize to meet needs without waiting for denominational headquarters to give permission or a publisher to tell them how to do it.

Vineyard Community Church in Cincinnati sometimes advertises their church as "A 12 Step Recovery Community." The church announces a threefold commitment to addicted people seeking recovery: "To be safe for each other, to be accepting of each other, to be responsible for ourselves." Vineyard offers support and recovery groups "for those seeking Christ-centered healing for psychological, emotional, and spiritual wounds." Their elaborate "Welcome" brochure for visitors explains that "the primary goal of the recovery groups is revealing the truth. In these groups we are exposed to affirming relationships, the Word, the Holy Spirit and time . . . all necessary to provide healing." Vineyard leaders believe that the 12 Steps

> have been given by God to provide us with a spiritual framework for recovery, a path to follow to wholeness, and a means by which to hold ourselves and each other accountable to that process. In the searching light of the Twelve Steps, we focus on the reality of our lives and of our relationships with God, with ourselves, and with others. If we persevere in working this program, we inevitably find that God is changing our lives, and that we are truly recovering. . . .
>
> The promise of 12 Step recovery is that if we are diligent about taking these steps, we will be amazed at how God meets our attempts with unexplainable success. We are going to know a new freedom and a new happiness. We will not regret the past nor wish to shut the door on it. We will comprehend the word serenity and we will know a peace that is difficult to explain. No matter how far down the scale we have gone, we will see how our experience can benefit others. The feeling of uselessness and self-pity will disappear. We will lose interest in selfish things and gain interest in others. Self-seeking behavior will slip away. Our whole attitude and outlook on life will change. Fear of people and situations will leave us. We will intuitively know how to handle situations which used to baffle us. We will suddenly realize that God is doing for us what we could not do for ourselves.
>
> Are these extravagant promises? *We think not!* They are being fulfilled among us—sometimes quickly, sometimes slowly. . . .

In addition to the kind of groups frequently found for alcohol and drug recovery, anger management, divorce recovery, grief support, sexual abuse, codependency, and so on, Vineyard offers support groups for battered women, head injury trauma support, job loss/career planning support, men's sexuality support, men's thought life struggles, depression recovery, and weight loss support.

Willow Creek Community Church has pioneered, within its "Community Care Ministries," several support and recovery ministries which will complete our survey of this movement. They offer the following rationale for these ministries:

> The overarching philosophy of Community Care begins with the fact that people matter to God. "The Lord is close to the brokenhearted and saves those who are crushed in spirit" (Psalm 34:18 NIV).
>
> All people encounter problems from time to time that hinder spiritual and/or emotional growth. These problems may result from a crisis, unwise choices, ignorance of life principles, improper development in childhood and/or chemical imbalance, personal sin, the effects of others' sins, or the result of spiritual testing or discipline.
>
> Whatever the cause, God calls the church to be an agent of healing and support for those going through times of crisis or need.[28]

A typical week at Willow Creek involves about 350 people, many relating to the following addiction groups: AA, Al-Anon (families of alcoholics), Al-Ateen (teenagers of alcoholics), Al-Akids (children, ages 6-12, of alcoholics), NA (Narcotics Anonymous), EA (Emotions Anonymous), OA (Overeaters Anonymous), SA (Sexaholics Anonymous), S-Anon (families of SA), and Co-DA (Codependents Anonymous).

Several other Willow Creek support group ministries are distinctive: The Rebuilders ministry "provides biblical insight and relational support to those who have experienced marital breakdown, in order to bring them to a resolution that honors God."[29] The program begins with an eight-week workshop. The last two sessions separate persons who will attempt marital restoration into one group, and those for whom divorce is certain or actual into the other. These two groups then continue as weekly support groups. "Oasis" is a support group ministry for children whose parents are working on marital reconciliation or divorce recovery in the Rebuilders ministry. Willow Creek has observed that

> the children of parents in marital breakdown have a heightened need to meet and interact with other children their own ages who are in similar family situations. This provides the children with the assurance that their situation is not so unusual and they are not "abnormal." . . . Children often act out

things that trouble them that they cannot express. This is especially true in Oasis. The focus of this ministry is to help children deal constructively with these overwhelming feelings.

I suggest that the 12 Step recovery group movement will one day be regarded as "The Underground Revival" of the 1990s and the early-twenty-first century. As I observe churches and interview first-generation believers, far more people are experiencing the saving grace of God through the 12 Step movement than through any other single type of outreach.

Church leaders who are considering joining this movement, however, need one dose of realism. New Hope's Dale Galloway reminds us that you cannot build a church capable of reaching and servicing the many needy, struggling, and dysfunctional people and families out there by targeting them alone. They will drain a church leader's energy and a church's finances, and many of them may never be in a position to prosper, pay their way, and support the expanded level of staff, facilities, and programming that it takes to serve more people like them, much less reach a city. So, Galloway admits, "We also invite, and welcome, successful people who share our vision."[30]

Small Groups in Perspective

All of the apostolic congregations I have studied place a great emphasis on what happens to people through small group dynamics. Frazer Memorial United Methodist Church's small groups achievement is less obvious than some because they build upon a Sunday school that, in average attendance, is the largest in their denomination. While some Sunday school classes are large teaching classes, those classes are divided into smaller groups for some connecting, nurture, prayer, and ministry to each other.

The Community Church of Joy may involve more people in small group life than any other Lutheran church in North America. The Ginghamsburg United Methodist Church, with a membership approaching 1,000, involves almost 1,200 people in small groups!

New Song Church continues this movement by involving its "Buster" membership in more than 100 groups. The church is clear that its four core "values" (defined as "the non-negotiable parameters of our ministry") are:

• Prayer and Worship
• Creativity
• Small Groups
• Life and Leadership Development

Small groups are indispensable in the philosophy of New Song's leaders. They advance this rationale: "Because we believe that a small group of Christians and pre-Christians is the best place for disciple making, edification, equipping, accountability, and growth, we will encourage all aspects of our ministry to be cell-based."

After eight years of history as a congregation, New Song has 105 groups meeting weekly; a dozen are recovery and support groups. Some of these groups target problems we would, by now, expect—people with alcohol addiction, or codependency, or desiring recovery from grief, divorce, low self-esteem, or compulsive anger. Others, however, represent imaginative local church responses—such as groups for people desiring recovery from homosexuality, or sex abuse, or spiritual abuse.

Small Groups are not, of course, universally applauded. Many churches and church leaders have not yet discovered the power and promise of the group movement. Many pastors of smaller churches prefer, and feel called, to do all the shepherding themselves. Many pastors (and staff) of larger churches are reluctant to move the church into small groups because "things might get out of hand!" As I emphasized in beginning this chapter, many agendas (of varying worth) can be pursued through the small group. For example, Flavil Yeakley has researched a genre of small group ministry in which group leaders appear to exercise inordinate control over the lives of their group members.[31]

Robert Wuthnow's *Sharing the Journey* publishes the results of a comprehensive three-year study, by a team of fifteen scholars, of the small group movement in America.[32] Wuthnow's research concludes that four out of every ten persons in the U.S. are involved in some kind of ongoing small group, and that this movement is quietly having a very major impact—not only upon the people involved in groups, but also upon the whole culture's understanding of community and the transcendent.

Wuthnow and his colleagues are generally favorable to small groups, but their critique uncovers some trade-offs and shortcomings in many small group ministries, and some of their critique is relevant to the two structures (cell and celebration) that I have claimed are basic to apostolic congregations. For instance, Wuthnow believes that small groups *ought* to be more heterogeneous (by culture, race, gender, and age) than affinity-based small groups usually are![33] Again, people seem to acquire through small group experience more of a sense of intimacy with God than of the transcendence and majesty of God.[34]

It is unrealistic and counterproductive, however, to expect small groups to achieve *everything* worthwhile, especially when our other structure—the large Christian celebration—is more likely to be heterogeneous, and more able to convey a sense of God's transcendence. Professor Wuthnow, how-

113

ever, unfortunately characterizes the churches that feature large celebrations as "megachurches." He believes that very large churches are the products of pride and ministerial ambition, that "the megachurch concept of thousands of people jammed like sardines into a huge auditorium bears no relation at all to the real level at which community is found," and he believes that the groups in megachurches "are reduced to being muscles in the great growth monster."[35]

In this writer's hyperbole (quite unlike the more objective and scientific language in most of the book), we are reminded of F. D. Maurice's observation that most people "are right in what they affirm, and wrong in what they deny."

In any case, some sociologists take a different view of these same matters. In 1977, I interviewed Professor David Martin, an esteemed sociologist of religion—then teaching at the London School of Economics, and also a British Methodist lay preacher. I asked him, "What in the lore of the sociology of religion should inform the evangelization approach of a large denomination?" After commenting that no denominational executive had ever asked him such a question before, he offered "two conclusions with confidence."

First, he said that all Christians and pre-Christian seekers should be yoked in small groups—for scripture study, sharing, prayer, accountability, support, and mutual empowerment. There are some things that people need, he said, that if they do not experience them in small groups—they do not experience them. Second, he said that the large Christian rally or celebration is an idea whose time has come again. He spoke of the vision, strength, hope, and contagion that are uniquely available in the large celebration.[36] The early church and the early Methodists knew these two principles; a generation of "apostolic congregations" are now demonstrating them once again.

Undoubtedly, three of the obvious criteria for evaluating small groups ministry in an "apostolic" project would center around reached people, changed lives, and effective lay pastoral care. While my data from the churches is especially rich on these points, one case in Willow Creek's small groups ministries is fairly typical.

Dennis, a husband and father in his early forties, works for an airline in downtown Chicago. A couple of years ago, his eleven-year-old son was struggling at home and school, and was hospitalized with what was then misdiagnosed as "attention deficit disorder." As Dennis watched his boy through a hospital window his "illusion of being in control" came crashing down. "I realized I could not control the outcome, and there wasn't much in my life I could control." He tried to pray, saying, "God, get us through this and I will walk the straight and narrow." In this same season, he injured his arm at work and went to see a physical therapist, Ashley, who attends Willow Creek and had Willow Creek literature in her office. He commented to his wife that evening that "something is wrong with the physical therapist. No one is that nice. No one cares that much." When he mentioned the Willow Creek materials, his wife recalled that she had attended the church several times when it met in a theater.

They telephoned Ashley; she and her husband took Dennis and his wife to a Willow Creek Seeker Service. "It was my first time in church in fifteen years," Dennis said. The drama that morning related to his son's problem, "and it blew me away. After the service, I was knocking people down to get saved." Bill Hybels advised Dennis to come back several times and test this urge. "I committed to Christ two weeks later, and my wife decided to follow Jesus two days later."

One weekend he attended a camp for fathers and sons. Meeting in a group with four other dads, he asked them to pray for his son, and for his healing. "God and that group gave us strength as a family." When his boy was finally diagnosed as manic-depressive and returned to the hospital, "The guys called an emergency meeting, and laid hands on me, and prayed for us for an hour and a half." Dennis reports, "I cannot emphasize enough what the love and support of a group has meant to us. This is the church. Groups are the church. Care is the church. The main emphasis is upon the heart." His son is better, though not yet well, "but he loves to come to the youth ministry. I see more love and care in this church than anywhere else in my world." Dennis now leads a men's group—each man with a son about the same age, and Dennis is helping an apprentice to become a group leader. The other four dads are now coaches in the men's ministry. The five men still meet some as a group. Dennis believes that "God put our men's group together."

There is no doubt that small groups, in which scripture, prayer, and nurture are experienced, do make a difference in people's lives. But do they, in fact, help prepare their group members for outreach and witness? My own interviews in churches have revealed that people who do engage in witness and inviting are *very* likely to be involved in a small group where people share their experiences and discuss the faith. This acquired facility for faith sharing then extends, somewhat naturally, into the other relationships of their life. I have also discovered that people who were *reached* by a small group are even more likely to extend the faith to others, in part because they have firsthand knowledge of the kind of group life to which they can invite people. One such man reports, "I can invite my neighbor to church, or to the empty chair in my group, or to a group for people with his problem!"

Robert Wuthnow's research confirmed this overall correlation between group life and witness. About 55 percent of group members, in Wuthnow's sampling, reported that group involvement enabled them to share their faith. Wuthnow reports that this is one of the several "huge" differences that group involvement makes in the lives of Christians.[37] The groups that study the Bible seem to influence the participant's faith the most, and also most enable group members to share their faith.[38] In addition to grounding people in some scripture and providing "practice" in faith discussion, Wuthnow identified another important factor in the group members' spiritual preparation for witness: the feeling of, or confidence in, one's own spiritual authenticity. Wuthnow explains:

> Group members . . . are trying to incorporate some sense of spirituality into their lives so that it will shine through naturally. They worry, like all modern people seem to, about appearing unauthentic. They don't want their neighbors to consider them phonies. The group, perhaps more than anything else, gives them confidence that their spirituality is connected with the way they live. It does this by providing verbal connections between private piety and some community of significant others. Thus, convinced that their faith is authentic, they feel that other people will be attracted to it naturally.[39]

Wuthnow adds an important insight that anticipates the last chapter of this book. Group-based people who do outreach "are not drawn to the formal programs of evangelism that many clergy advocate," nor especially to techniques or arguments, nor to becoming "a bubbly, smiling Christian with all the answers." Their approach is more natural and relational, and often has "a deeper and more sustained impact."[40]

So, effective groups prepare many of their members for outreach and witness, but not always. Sometimes, groups that meet a long time become closed circles, or cliques, whose members neither welcome new persons into the group nor engage in outreach beyond the group. To counter this long-term tendency, Cincinnati's Vineyard Community Church has pioneered a significant new norm for their 120 groups. Each group engages in periodic outreach, every four to six weeks, to pre-Christian people. Their senior pastor, Steve Sjogren, has observed that the group that reaches out thereby involves the shy members who lack the courage to reach out on their own.

Indeed, Sjogren contends that only a relatively small percentage of evangelical Christians ever do personal evangelism. Granting that "the common scenario (for doing evangelism) involves one lone individual sharing Christ with an unbeliever," he wagers "that effective and widespread outreach will not happen with individual Christians going out into the community. It is just too scary for most people to step out in this way." Vineyard has discovered "courage . . . in numbers" for doing evangelism.[41] This Vineyard church has also discovered that groups can reach some people that an individual cannot, and that the group that engages in periodic outreach becomes closer as a group.

So, for a range of reasons, we now know that involving most of a church's people in small groups contributes greatly to building an effective apostolic congregation.

CHAPTER FIVE

✝

How Lay Ministry Advances the Christian Movement

In the eleven o'clock Sunday morning service before Christmas last year, the people of a Lexington, Kentucky area church presented a Christmas gift to their pastor and his family. The pastor had especially helped one man in a crisis very recently, so that man was invited to present the gift, with this story.

One day in early December, the pastor arrived at the church shortly before eight in the morning. He prepared the bulletin for the next Sunday, wrote a draft for the next Sunday sermon, dictated some correspondence, spent three hours in conferences, then visited in homes for the remaining afternoon and the evening. At nine that evening, past time to call it a day, he "felt led" to visit one more home. The man of the home was distressed as he answered the door. Within the hour, a relative had telephoned—threatening to come over and shoot him! The pastor stepped into the gap, stood by the man, mediated between him and the caller, and finally went home a little before midnight—which was only a little later than the staff-parish relations committee informed him the church needed a pastoral change. One of the several reasons given was that the members did not feel like they were receiving adequate pastoral care!

The committee rightly concluded that the members were not receiving adequate pastoral care. However, they wrongly assumed that (within a "traditional church" paradigm) people can receive adequate pastoral care; and they were certainly wrong in concluding that it was the pastor's "fault." With the possible exception of some small churches, not many people get adequate pastoral care from their pastor. It may once have been possible, but with the people's "maxed out" calendars and the expanded job description of every pastor, it is no longer possible.

Associate Pastor Rick Martinez, of New Hope Community Church, invites pastors to ask this question to the leadership group in their traditional church: "Do you think that enough of our people are getting the right kind of pastoral care?" He advises, "They will say 'no,' so don't feel insecure when they say it. Feel free to agree with them. They will be surprised when you agree!"

My own research produces three conclusions close to Martinez's conclusion. First, I am in many traditional churches in which the people seem to get adequate crisis pastoral care; if you have emergency surgery, or if your loved one dies, the pastor will be there. But, in traditional churches virtually no one gets adequate, ongoing, "regular," week-by-week (or month-by-month, or season-by-season) pastoral care. Second, better-than-adequate crisis care depends upon a relationship that is established only through regular pastoral care.

Third, regular pastoral care (much more than crisis care) is an important producer of a people who share their faith. Most Christians who share their faith and invite others to Christ and the Church are themselves in regular spiritual conversation and prayer with a significant other who serves as their pastor. Most of the Christians who do not share and invite are not regularly pastored by anyone. Welcome to yet another crisis in contemporary Christianity: most people in most churches do not receive regular pastoral care, and this is yet another cause of the stagnation of traditional churches.

There is, however, an abundantly proven solution to this problem—as suggested in the following story.

Biblical Precedents for Lay Ministries

Jack Rogers, who taught philosophy of religion at Fuller Theological Seminary, once helped me "rediscover" lay ministry. In a presentation to Presbyterians in California, Rogers alluded favorably to the ordination of women. In the following question and answer session, one fellow challenged the speaker "to justify the ordination of women, biblically." I will never forget Jack Rogers' response: "I will be glad to justify the ordination of women biblically when *you* have justified the ordination of *men* biblically. Or the ordination of *anyone* biblically! Early Christianity was a *lay movement. No one* was 'ordained' in the sense that any Christian tradition means it today." Rogers explained that ordination of some people to the priesthood is a postcanonical development within the Church. It is a product of the Traditions, but not of the New Testament.

Jack Rogers was right, of course. Jesus and the apostles all "bypassed seminary." They never met the educational and ecclesiastical requirements that would have credentialed them to be priests within Judaism. The early Christian movement exploded and developed without regard to any set-apart priesthood. God's new People, as a body, constituted a "holy" and "royal priesthood" (1 Peter 2:5, 9). According to Paul, the Holy Spirit gifted some people to be apostles, and others prophets, teachers, miracle workers, healers, helpers, administrators, evangelists, pastors, and so on "to equip the saints for the work of ministry, for building up the body of Christ" (see 1 Corinthians 12:28 and Ephesians 4:11-12).

So, there are many ministries, and everyone is gifted for some ministry. The Body of Christ needs all the ministries, so one ministry is not more important than another. We are called out from the world to be a people in ministry to one another and to the world. The New Testament did not inflict upon us this artificial and tragic split between the clergy and the laity, the professionals and the amateurs, the players and the spectators.

Reformation Precedents for Lay Ministries

This biblical truth about "the priesthood of all believers" was one of the major discoveries of the Protestant Reformation. Kenneth Scott Latourette explains the view of Martin Luther:

> Luther held that ordination had been invented by the Church of Rome. He admitted that as a rite practiced for many ages it was not to be condemned, but he reiterated as one of his basic convictions that all Christians are priests, that what is called priesthood is merely a ministry entrusted to those who exercise it with the consent of other Christians, and that ordination is a ceremony for choosing preachers in the Church. As imposed by Rome, he said, the sacrament of ordination made for a separation of clergy and laity and the tyranny of the former over the latter. . . . While not altogether sweeping aside or deprecating vows, Luther found no ground in Scripture for those of perpetual poverty, chastity, and obedience which are taken by monks and nuns. . . . He maintained that the works of priests and members of the religious orders are not a whit more sacred in the sight of God than those of a farmer in his fields or of a woman in her household duties.[1]

Contemporary writers on lay ministry usually assume that the Reformation delivered to its people an authoritative and accessible scripture, and justification by grace through faith alone, but that the Reformation never delivered on its promise of the Priesthood of All Believers; somehow, that doctrine never became operative. They assume, therefore, that "we live in the generation when the unfinished business of the Reformation may at last be completed."[2]

However, there was at least one branch of the Reformation—eighteenth-century Methodism—that *did* fulfill the doctrine and made it as operative as anyone is calling for today. We need to insert this fact into the record, not only to check this generation's conceit and to mollify nostalgic Methodists, but also to demonstrate that what is being proposed today has already been done before, on a very wide scale and with the kind of revolutionary impact that is dreamed of today.

John Wesley came to perceive that the Holy Spirit has gifted many lay-people for all sorts of ministries. Within a year or two after his 1738 Aldersgate experience, Wesley had a movement on his hands, with much need for outreach, teaching, ministry, and leadership—with virtually no ordained clergy at his disposal. The only people available were gifted lay-people.

Wesley did not stampede toward the lay solution, but he had experiential warrant for considering it. As an impressionable boy, he had observed for months the undeniable power of a growing Sunday evening ministry of his own mother, Susanna, as up to 200 people assembled in, and outside, her Epworth kitchen. She later influenced John to the conclusion that Thomas Maxfield, and presumably other laypeople, were called by God to preach. Early, he observed the blessing of God attending the ministries and witness of many Methodist laypeople.

So Wesley evolved into the understanding that the Church's ministry to Christians, and to non-Christians, is primarily entrusted to the laity. While several other traditions, including the Church of England, had some laity involved in some ministries and causes, Methodism quickly "out laicized" the other denominations and became essentially a lay movement.

Laypeople did virtually all the ministry that took place in, and out from, every Methodist society. There were class leaders, and band leaders, and other kinds of small group leaders, as well as local preachers and those so-called "assistants" who took de facto charge of societies and circuits—all laypersons. Other laypeople visited sick and hospitalized people; others worked with children and their families; others visited poor people, widows, and single parent families; still others engaged in conversations with undiscipled people and started new classes for seekers.

Wesley did not leave to chance the organization of lay ministries. Leaders selected people for various ministries with care. Each ministry had a "job description." People were "developed" for various roles. Their performance was observed and "coached." Moreover, in Methodism's unique marriage of ministry and evangelism, everyone who ministered also evangelized. Wesley knew what the church growth movement has (re)discovered—that most of the Christians who regularly share their faith are Christians involved in some ministry, and who experience God working through their ministry. So, the priority objective of class leaders, sick visitors and the other laity in ministry was to "save souls."

Of course, the early Methodist societies had preachers, but it would be easy to exaggerate their status and importance. They served "circuits" of several societies, and they itinerated every year or two; in any case, the vast majority of them were nonordained lay preachers. It is true that, in time, the preachers—through their annual conference—governed the connection. The laity were not involved in high level ecclesiastical politics, but their time and energy were thereby freed for ministries in societies and communities.

Wesley believed in the movement's, and the people's, possibilities. He challenged his leaders to read, learn, and develop, and he believed they could be the agents for a great movement of the Spirit. Wesley may have overestimated the gifts and capacities of his people; Gordon Rupp once commented that "Wesley's geese were too often swans in his eyes." But a lay movement Methodism was, a Protestant movement that went quite beyond "priesthood of all believers" sloganeering and actually entrusted virtually all the ministry that matters to laypeople. Methodism was a "lay apostolate" before we knew what to call it.

I cannot deny that Methodism eventually abandoned its own distinctive identity as a lay movement and became *at least* as entrenched in the dysfunctional clergy-laity heresy as any other Christian tradition. Decades ago, as Methodists sought the respectability of the Presbyterians and Episcopalians, the tradition shifted its accent from lay ministry to professional ministry. Methodist clergy and laity today are much more likely to regard their parish as their world than the world as their parish! Nevertheless, historic Methodism stands as one model, historically achieved and enduring for generations, of the ministry and mission of the laity. What we propose today is no unproved theoretical pipe dream!

For a long time, some leaders and analysts within the denominations have called for the recovery of lay ministry in our lifetime, but prophetic preachments and books on the theology of the laity have made little enduring difference. Most church leaders have not known what to do—beyond theological reflection and public advocacy; it is one thing to want the priesthood of all believers to be a reality, but another thing to see it realized. We have experienced a lot of "hand-wringing" over this dilemma.

In recent years, however, a growing number of bellwether congregations have experienced significant breakthroughs in recovering lay ministry and a lay apostolate. Their pioneering is demonstrating reproducible ways forward for many other congregations. In these churches, I have observed two effective models for engaging and deploying many laity; I call them the Volunteer Model and the Seminar Model.

The Volunteer Model: Frazer Memorial United Methodist Church

Frazer Memorial United Methodist Church, in Montgomery, Alabama, is a 7,500 member church that involves over 83 percent of its resident members in over 190 lay ministries. Frazer's approach to the deployment of laypeople in ministry is based on a number of distinctives and innovations.

The first of two central principles in Frazer's system is volunteerism. Most traditional churches "recruit" people to serve in various jobs in the church—often recruiting "square pegs" to fit into "round holes." In some cases, church leaders recruit mere names to "fill slots" in an annual report to the judicatory to show that all the prescribed offices and jobs are "covered." When pastors or other church leaders recruit people for an office or a job, many people are compliant enough to say "Yes" to tasks for which they are not gifted or interested; their performance is virtually always less than their best.

The Church is learning what the U.S. government has learned—that you get much better performance from a volunteer army than from a force of draftees. John Ed Mathison, senior pastor at Frazer, believes that the volunteer approach to lay ministry is much more effective, for several reasons: Individual people are much more likely to have an intuitive sense of their abilities and giftedness than are the leaders who would recruit many people at a time. When people volunteer for a task, they have greater ownership, with greater follow-through, with greater performance and excellence. The volunteer system takes advantage of people's strongest interests, and it affirms their talents and giftedness.[3]

Frazer's chief method for helping people volunteer for a ministry involves the circulation, every November, of a "Ministry Menu" of (the last I checked) some 190 options for getting involved in a ministry for the next calendar year. Leaders encourage people to indicate first and second choices on the ministry menu; this enables the leaders to place a sufficient number of people in most of the ministries on the menu. Training for ministries then takes place in January of the new year. A person's commitment is for one year; many people renew their commitment to the same ministry, year after year. Frazer's leaders communicate the expectation that every member will be involved in a ministry. (If you do not like any of the 190 ministry options on the Menu, number 191 is a blank—in which you write in a ministry you would help start!) When new members join the church, the orientation session for new members has one fundamental agenda: to secure, using the Ministry Menu, their involvement in a ministry.

What if, in November, not enough people sign up for a ministry? This may indicate that God has not led enough persons to volunteer for that ministry, so maybe Frazer should not be engaged in that ministry. Mathison explains that

> an important ministry should not be discontinued immediately if an insufficient number of people volunteer to serve in it. If, for example, no one volunteered on the ministry menu in November to serve as parking lot ushers, the congregation should be informed of this and given a second opportunity to volunteer in this area. If no one responds at this time, then the church needs to have a good funeral service for a ministry that is no longer needed. A funeral service will be far more effective than trying to recruit people to do something that they really don't want to do just in order to continue a ministry that functioned last year.

In Frazer's approach, it is not primarily the responsibility of staff to do ministry (though the staff are "playing coaches"), but to train, coach, and facilitate the ministry and mission of the church's lay army. The staff has developed some notable approaches to facilitating lay ministry. One approach stresses recognition for persons involved in lay ministries. Mathison and the staff, in my observation, never take much credit for what Frazer achieves; they commend the laity who do the ministry. Frazer publishes *Frazer Family News* each month. This quality "Christian tabloid" usually features, with pictures, the ministries of Frazer's laity. Many articles read like an extension of the book of the Acts of the Apostles.

Another facilitation approach involves the frequent use of testimony. For example, many church services feature a layperson who speaks briefly on what God is doing through his or her ministry. As people greet one another at the designated time in the worship service, people frequently are invited to shake hands, give their names, and tell the ministry in which they are involved. Again, Frazer's committee meetings often have a time on the agenda for a couple of people to tell what God is doing through their ministry. Each meeting of the church's Administrative Board and its Council on Ministries features a person who reports on his or her ministry and what it means to him or her.

The overall effect is contagious. The act of testifying reinforces people's commitment to their ministries, and gives them public practice in verbalizing their experiences. As people who are not yet involved in a ministry hear from so many other people who are, this communicates the importance of Frazer Church's norm that everyone be involved in a ministry, and encourages them to enlist. The practice also appeals to visitors who are open to a church where laity can make their lives count. The climate that all of this creates has one other consequence: Frazer experiences less internal conflict than any other church I know. Mathison explains: "People who are rowing the boat don't have time to rock the boat!"

If the first major principle in Frazer's philosophy of ministry is *voluntarism*, the second is *meeting needs;* and this principle has opened the way for an "entrepreneurial laity." The history of Frazer Memorial United Methodist Church is largely a history of the multiplication of ministries, and most of Frazer's new ministries are a response to unmet human need. The church's Council on Ministries evaluates all programs and ministries, and all proposals for new programs and ministries, with two questions:

1) Does it meet a need?
2) Does it make disciples?

The church has discovered that you do not best implement this philosophy by "importing" programs from denominational headquarters. While Frazer often draws from the best denominational and parachurch resources they can find, the program that is locally developed is usually the most effective. Frazer believes that involving laity in ministries—for which they volunteered, that actually meet people's needs—prevents the "burnout" we observe in many laity in many churches.

Frazer Church has three methods for discovering needs for which ministries need developing. First, Frazer has a lay task force whose members research and network the city to discover unmet needs. For example, this task force's discovery of the number of preschool and elementary-age children in Frazer's ministry area informed the need for a weekday kindergarten at Frazer for four- and five-year-old children, and the need for an expanded approach to children's worship on Sundays. By the late 1980s, Frazer was featuring twelve children's worship services at 9:40 A.M.! Again, the task force discovered an extensive need for singles ministries, which led to Frazer developing the largest singles ministry in the city.

The second method by which Frazer discovers needs is exercised when individual members, through their networks of contacts in the city, discover needs and report them to the church. The third method is item 191 on the Ministry Menu—where people write in a ministry they would volunteer to help start.

Frazer church has learned that through recognizing the gifts and abilities of the laity and implementing the principle of voluntarism, the laity can be liberated and fulfilled and the church can become a local movement. Frazer has also discovered the great cost-effectiveness of a lay approach to ministry. Mathison explains:

By involving laity in ministry rather than hiring professionals to do ministry, you can be responsible about the stewardship of financial resources. Every member in ministry multiplies the results of ministry at far less cost to the local church. While most churches with 3,000 plus members spend 40 to 55 percent of their expenditures for staff salaries and benefits, Frazer spends about 30 percent for staff.[4]

The Seminar Model: Willow Creek and Saddleback Valley

While the Volunteer model assumes that people will know intuitively and/or by the Spirit's lead what ministry to enlist for, the Seminar model assumes that many people need more or better self-insight before they are ready to commit to a ministry, and that training, with self-assessment tools, can achieve this self-insight and facilitate an informed decision.

Willow Creek Community Church's "Network" approach is worth considering. The church has 6,000 people involved in 4,500 roles serving in 90 ministries. The Network resources that have informed the meaningful placement of so many people are now available from Zondervan, which makes Willow Creek's training approach very available to other churches. Many of their assumptions are similar to Frazer's—that all Christians are gifted for some ministry; that when people serve out of their giftedness and strengths, they are more effective, and the Body of Christ is edified; that people need meaningful places of service to be fulfilled as Christian disciples. Willow Creek further believes that people need to discover more about who they are, and they need an organized process to help them develop into effective servants. The goal of their process is to deploy "the right people . . . in the right places . . . for the right reasons." Their process involves three phases: teaching, consultation, and service.

The form of the *teaching* phase is an eight-hour seminar designed, essentially, to help people discover (1) their "Passion"—which indicates where they will serve, (2) their "Spiritual Gifts"—which indicates what they will do in ministry, and (3) their "Personal Style"—which indicates how they will serve. Willow Creek believes that all Christians are called to serve the Kingdom based on their "Servant Profile," that is, the composite of their Passion, Personal Gifts, and Personal Style.

In one session, the Network seminar teaches that our ministry-related passion (or conviction, or burden, or sense of call) is "the God given desire that compels us to make a difference in a particular ministry." People move toward clarifying their passion by filling out their "Passion Assessment" instrument. Several questions on the instrument call for participants to complete a statement. One of several is: "At the end of my life, I'd love to

be able to look back and know that I'd done something about:_____
_____."

    Two other probes are multiple choice. The participant identifies, among 21 options (such as children, young marrieds, elderly people, teen moms, single parents, and prisoners), "the people I would most like to help." The participant also identifies, among 24 options (such as family, education, injustice, hunger, AIDS, reaching the lost) "the issues or causes I feel strongly about." Still another probe invites people to list the top five to seven experiences they have had in their life and briefly describe what they did and why it was meaningful to them. This exercise usually helps people uncover a theme from their life experiences that gives insight into their Passion. People complete the session by working together in "huddle groups."

    The Network seminar devotes three sessions to teaching the doctrine of Spiritual Gifts and helping participants discover their gifts. Our spiritual gifts are the special abilities that the Holy Spirit imparts within us according to God's purpose for us. One or more gifts are entrusted to us to use in faithful ministry and to edify the body of believers. As a body of diverse individuals, we each have different gifts; we depend on one another's gifts for the whole work of the church's ministry. The second session on gifts walks the participant through eight biblical passages that feature spiritual gifts, through which the reader is introduced, inductively, to the 23 gifts that are mentioned in scripture. Participants then work through an instrument to determine their probable giftedness. These discoveries still need to be tested in ministry involvement, and they need to be confirmed by the body. A third session affirms the importance of doing ministry based on our strengths, and shows people how to link their gifts with their passion and helps them begin to identify the kinds of ministry they should consider.

    The sixth session introduces the role of love and servanthood in lay ministry. The seventh session helps people identify their God-given *personal style*. One continuum, asking "How are you energized?" helps participants determine whether they are more task oriented or people oriented. The other continuum, asking "How are you organized?" helps participants determine whether they are more unstructured or structured. Participants then discover that their personal style is in one of four quadrants:

Task/Unstructured   Task/Structured
People/Unstructured   People/Structured

Having clarified *how* a person serves, the session concludes with additional insights on the kind of position or role in which the participant might best serve. The eighth session considers variables like the person's degree of availability for ministry (considering work, family, and other responsibilities and constraints), and the person's spiritual maturity, to prepare each person for a conference with a "consultant"—whose ministry is helping other people get placed in a ministry. The seminar ends with important theological affirmations like the following:

> Before all of creation, God prepared some ministry opportunities for you to do. God created you. He sent Jesus Christ to make a relationship possible with you. He called you. He saved you. He gave you his Holy Spirit. He gave you a Spiritual Gift. He gave you the power of the Spirit to minister to the body with that gift. He identified the works he wants you to do. He put a passion in your heart. He gave you a personal style. He promises his continued activity and presence. Is there anything else God could do?[5]

Willow Creek's leaders confess that "to our amazement, people really are willing to spend all of this time just to find out where they should serve."[6] Willow Creek takes about 150 people per month through the Network seminar. Of those who meet with their consultant, approximately 85 percent are placed into a ministry.

Saddleback Valley Community Church has emphasized lay ministry since Rick Warren planted the church in 1980. Rick Warren reports that, in a traditional church, only 10 percent of all laypersons are active in a ministry; an additional 40 percent would *like* to be involved in ministry *but* either have never been asked or don't know how! This data quickly dramatizes what is possible for a church in lay ministry—if it will free the laity's time from committee work, maintenance, and governance, and, with training, authorize and empower the mission of the laity. Over 1,000 Saddleback members are involved in serious, demanding, avocational ministries; several hundred members serve each year in short-term, overseas, cross-culture mission experiences. In their fifteen-year history, Saddleback's people have helped plant 24 daughter congregations!

Saddleback's emphasis on lay ministry is the single greatest key to the church's success. Rick Warren explains that, for their church, "The people are the ministers, and the pastors are the administers." The staff make most of the necessary administrative decisions, thus freeing the laity from the consuming involvements in committee work, voting, governance, and maintenance that immobilize, divide, and exhaust most congregations. This frees the people's time and energy for ministry and outreach in the community. The staff's key role is to "lead and feed" the laity, thereby "equipping the saints" for their ministries.

The church begins where people are, and manages a "Life Development" process for helping people become serving and reproductive Christians. Warren developed a "baseball diamond" analogy, which he teaches to the people to guide their development. "First base" involves a commitment to membership, "second base" to maturity, "third base" to ministry, and "fourth base" to mission. Each of these milestones is facilitated through a four-hour seminar (referred to as #101, #201, #301, and #401). People are invited at the end of each seminar to commit their lives around the seminar's focus.

Rick Warren believes that the great question confronting most pastors is "how to turn an audience into an army," so the church's #301 seminar on ministry is crucial to Saddleback's total strategy. The chief assumption behind Saddleback's approach is consistent with that of Frazer and Willow Creek—that you do not recruit people effectively by forcing square pegs into round holes. Most traditional churches first define a range of jobs, and then recruit people to fill each one, whether they "fit" or not. That may elicit compliance (if they like you they will say "OK"), but not performance.

In lay ministry, Warren believes, function should follow form. Therefore, you first discover how people are "shaped," and then help place them into a ministry or role that is right for their "shape." The word *shape* serves as an acronym for Saddleback's approach to helping people discover who they are and, therefore, where they would best serve. The #301 seminar on ministry helps people to find ministries and roles based on their *s*piritual gifts, *h*eart, *a*bilities, *p*ersonality, and *e*xperiences. The seminar explains that one's ministry should be determined by one's makeup, that when people are serving from their shape they are effective and experience fulfillment.

> What God made me to *be* determines what *he* intends me to *do*. I will understand the purpose I was created for when I understand the kind of person I am. This is the secret of knowing God's will for my life.

God is consistent in his plan for each of our lives. He would not give us inborn talents and temperaments, spiritual gifts, and all sorts of life experiences and then not use them! By reviewing and studying these factors, we can discover the ministry God has for us, . . . the unique way God intends for us to serve him.[7]

The seminar then proceeds to help each participant discover his or her unique S.H.A.P.E.

The seminar begins by helping people discover their **spiritual gifts** for ministry within and beyond the Body of Christ. Saddleback's leaders acknowledge that the understanding of spiritual gifts is not uniform or systematic in the New Testament; the several lists of gifts vary from one another and, presumably, they are not exhaustive. Furthermore, the doctrine of spiritual gifts is not a "heavyweight" doctrine; it lacks the "explanatory power" of, say, the doctrine of the Trinity. (For example, I have never met anyone who discovered, from filling out a spiritual gifts questionnaire, that they had the gift of "hospitality" who hadn't rather known that already!) Nevertheless, a spiritual gifts exercise can help a Christian to clarify what his or her several gifts probably are, and consider their "gift mix," and begin ministering with this clearer self-perception. Saddleback's leadership has observed, however, that people discover their gifts with greater certainty from experiences in ministry. The seminar manual names and explains 23 different gifts and gives people the opportunity to explore their possible gifts, as illustrated in the spiritual gift of Evangelism:

Evangelism
The ability to communicate the Good News of Jesus Christ to unbelievers in a positive, non-threatening way. The ability to sense opportunities to share Christ and lead people to respond with faith.

(   ) I'm pretty sure I have this gift.
(   ) I may have this gift.
(   ) I don't think I have this one.

During the seminar, participants pencil in their best self-perception about each of the gifts; later they will test the perceptions with several Christian friends who know them well.

The seminar unit on **"heart"** helps people to clarify their driving motivations, what Willow Creek calls their "passion." The seminar makes a profound theological point by assuming *congruence* between people's interests, passions, and motivations on the one hand, and the will of God on the other. "God had a purpose in giving you your inborn interests." (By contrast, many traditional churches and Christians assume that whatever God calls us to do must be contrary to our interests—implying, theologically, that what the Third Person calls us to do is inconsistent with how the First Person created us!) The seminar notes affirm that

God has given each of us a unique emotional heartbeat that races when we encounter activities, subjects, or circumstances that interest us. We instinctively feel deeply about some things and not about others.

This God-given motivation serves as an internal guidance system for our lives. It determines what your interests are, and what will bring you the most satisfaction and fulfillment. It also motivates you to pursue certain activities, subjects, and environments.[8]

Participants then process and clarify their interests in the following exercise: First, they list their accomplishments—defined as things they enjoyed doing and did well, in each decade of their life to date. Then they study their list of accomplishments to discover some common motivational thread(s). This enables them to identify two or three of the following possible motivators as their driving motives: I love to . . .

- design/Develop—starting or making something from scratch.
- pioneer—try out new concepts, even risking failure.
- organize—organizing something that is already started.
- operate/Maintain—something that is already organized.
- serve/Help—others succeed in their responsibility.
- acquire/Possess—as in shopping, obtaining, or collecting things, especially quality.
- excel—to be the best, to attain the highest standard.
- influence—as in shaping the beliefs, attitudes, and behaviors of others.
- perform—to be on stage, in the limelight.
- improve—taking something already started and making it better.
- repair—to fix what is broken or change what is out of date.
- lead/Be in charge—as in supervising, and determining what or how things will be done.
- persevere—as in persisting, and seeing things through to completion.
- follow the rules—as in operating by policies, and meeting organization's expectations.
- prevail—as in fighting for the right, opposing wrong, and overcoming injustice.

The session on **"abilities"** affirms that many of our skills and abilities, which we acquired genetically or in early experience, are as useful in the church's ministry as in the home or marketplace. The exercise refers participants to their earlier list of accomplishments and directs them to "circle all verbs that denote actions performed doing each achievement." The participant then compares those verbs to a list of "26 specialized abilities" that are especially useful in various aspects of church ministry—such as entertaining, recruiting, artistic, promoting, feeding, and decorating abilities, and people identify their strongest two or three.

The unit on **"personality"** encourages participants to minister in areas suited to their personalities, in ways consistent with how "God has wired your temperament." Then, building upon the well-known Myers-Briggs personality type questionnaires and other indicators of temperament, participants identify where they are in terms of five scales:

Extroverted 3 2 1 / 1 2 3 Introverted
Thinker 3 2 1 / 1 2 3 Feeler
Routine 3 2 1 / 1 2 3 Variety
Self-controlled 3 2 1 / 1 2 3 Self-expressive
Cooperative 3 2 1 / 1 2 3 Competitive

The final unit helps people to understand that God has also prepared them for ministry through their life **"experiences,"** particularly through their (1) educational, (2) vocational, (3) ministry, and (4) painful experiences. The most revolutionary of those claims is that God prepares us through the "hard knocks" and painful experiences of our lives, "that in all things God works for good in those who love him, who are called according to his purpose." Therefore, #301 class participants especially consider the possibility that God "wants you to be open to ministering to people who are going through what you have already been through." After participants record their important educational, vocational, ministry, and painful experiences, the four-hour seminar ends with a summary of insights and Saddleback's philosophy of ministry.

People then take their materials home and prayerfully fill out a "ministry profile" indicating their best estimate of their *shape;* they consider the perceptions of family members and Christian friends as they fill it out. They make an appointment with a lay ministry guide, who directs them to the three or four job descriptions (out of more than 200 job descriptions) that best match their shape, from which they prayerfully choose one. Saddleback now has over 1,000 laypersons who have experienced this four-hour seminar, who have discovered or clarified some important things about themselves, have committed their lives to lay ministry and mission, and are now serving in some ministry for which they are "shaped." Saddleback now places several hundred new laypersons, many of them new believers, in ministry each year. The many hundreds of members now involved in community ministries and witness account for the church's growing image as a "movement" in Orange County.

Laity as Shepherds

There are many lay ministries in a church. You will recall that Frazer Memorial United Methodist Church involves laity in some 190 ministries. No matter how many ministries a church's people are involved in, however, none is more crucial than the ongoing pastoral care of the People of God.

Apostolic congregations have an aversion to merely "winning" people (and building the church statistically) and then letting them fend for themselves. People worth winning are worth caring for. Furthermore, ongoing care keeps people connected, and feeling like they belong and they matter, and makes it possible to disciple them and move them toward their own ministry and mission. Saddleback's "baseball diamond" analogy for developing disciples serves as a good example of this point. The church's goal for people is to get them to first base (membership), then to second base (maturity directed), then to third base (ministry), and to fourth base (mission). Rick Warren explains that, like in baseball, "You don't get credit for people left on base!"

We began this chapter by suggesting that most people in most churches do not, and cannot, get adequate ongoing pastoral care from their pastor; crisis care yes, but ongoing care no. Christians need pastoral care when life is good, as well as when life is hard, but the pastor's expanded job description now makes it impossible for the pastor to be every member's personal chaplain. Few churches have, can afford, or can find enough ordained pastors and staff to go around. Every church, however, has enough people with the appropriate abilities and spiritual gifts to "shepherd a flock" within the church membership. We are learning that many lay people, with training, can do 90 percent of what an ordained pastor does. Lay people in great numbers can contact and encourage their people, love and care for them, listen to and empathize with them, engage in spiritual conversation with them, pray by their bed in the hospital, support them in loss and grief, and be generally watchful and available as a shepherd to the sheep.

We have already seen, in the chapter on small groups, that some churches like New Hope Community Church have their small group leaders also serve as the pastor of the people in their group. So New Hope has over 600 gifted and trained "lay pastors." Dale Galloway's *Ministry Skills for Small Group Leaders* (see the appendix, Selected Resources) is a good example for what is possible in preparing laity for pastoral care.

Saddleback Valley Community Church began like most churches—with the ordained pastor trying to do all the pastoring. When the church was four years old, and serving 500 to 600 people, Rick Warren hit "the wall."

> I was still doing all the preaching and teaching, all the praying and pastoring. I was still trying to do all the counseling and everything. I was absolutely running out of energy.
>
> One Wednesday night I confessed: "Folks, I've had it. I do not have the energy to keep up with the pace of this church. I can't do it. But, in the New Testament, God doesn't expect me to do it all. I am to equip you for your ministry."

"I will make you a deal. I am supposed to give myself to prayer and the ministry of the Word. If you will do the ministry of this church, people, I will make sure you are well fed. How about it?"

That night we kind of struck a deal and signed a covenant and shook hands with each other—that I would make sure the congregation was well fed and they would do the ministry. And the church exploded to a new level of growth, instantly.

Saddleback followed a similar model to New Hope's for years; the small group leader was also the lay pastor for the group members. However, they found it more difficult to recruit people for the "pastor" part of the job (many people gifted and interested in group leadership could not imagine themselves as "pastors"). They fell behind in the number of group leaders needed to expand their groups ministries, so they divided the roles. Nevertheless, Saddleback has well over 150 lay pastors serving their 4,200 adult members.

At Saddleback, the people whose *shape* suggests they would make good lay pastors are invited to the church's periodic Lay Pastor Institute. Rick Warren depends more upon on-the-job training and the church's monthly S.A.L.T. (Saddleback Advanced Leadership Training) events to train people than upon initial training. He contends that many churches "put out people's fire by overtraining them" in, say, a one-year course before they get to actually express their *shape* in some ministry. Nevertheless, the Institute is a good model for getting appropriately gifted people started.

Some of the major sessions of Saddleback's Lay Pastor Institute focus on the character qualifications of a lay pastor, the job description, the role of lay pastors within Saddleback's overall strategy, principles of hospital visitation, and an introduction to basic lay pastor skills. The session that focuses, from four biblical passages, on the heart of a pastor is especially noteworthy. Here is Rick Warren's complete outline of that presentation:

The Heart of a Pastor
by Pastor Rick Warren
"Poimen: The Shepherd!"
There are 4 key passages in the Bible that give us the characteristics of a good shepherd:

John 10:1-18, Psalm 23, Ezekiel 34:1-16, 1 Peter 5:2-4

Marks of an Effective Lay Pastor

135

John 10

1. A good shepherd *calls his sheep.* (v. 3)
2. A good shepherd *leads his sheep.* (v. 4*a*)
3. A good shepherd *knows his sheep.* (vv. 4*b*-5)
4. A good shepherd *makes sacrifices for his sheep.* (vv. 11-13)

Psalm 23

5. A good shepherd *meets needs.* (v. 1)
6. A good shepherd *provides guidance.* (vv. 2-3)
7. A good shepherd *gives comfort.* (v. 4)
8. A good shepherd *gives hope.* (vv. 5-6)

Ezekiel 34

9. A good shepherd *cares for the flock.* (vv. 2-3)
10. A good shepherd *strengthens the weak.* (v. 4*a*)
11. A good shepherd *seeks the lost.* (vv. 4*b*-10)

1 Peter 5

12. A good shepherd *is willing and eager.* (v. 2)
13. A good shepherd *is a good example.* (v. 3)

The reward: (v. 4)[9]

One day, a charter member of Saddleback Church had a heart attack. Rick Warren walked into the emergency room of a hospital to see him. Engaging the attention of the head nurse who looked very much in charge, he said, "I'm Pastor Rick, here to see Walt Stevens." The head nurse replied, "How many pastors does this church have? I'm sorry, you can't see him. Too many pastors have already seen him." Warren reports that she walked away, "and so I shot in anyway. It is often easier to get forgiveness than to get permission!" When the patient saw Warren, he exclaimed: "Pastor Rick, what are you doing here? I must really be sick! Five lay pastors have already visited me!" After a five-minute visit, Rick Warren walked away deeply moved and saying, "That is the way God meant for the church to operate. God never meant it to be a one-man show—here a prayer, there a prayer, everywhere a prayer prayer. God works through the ministry of the laity, and they have the right to know that God is working in their life."

Although Frazer Memorial United Methodist Church has involved lay-people in a wide range of ministries since the 1970s, the church did not begin its "lay minister" emphasis until 1988. Despite their strong Sunday school and a "redundant" system of caring in place, the leaders realized they needed laypeople engaging in basic pastoral care.

Frazer did not attempt to reinvent this wheel. Executive Pastor Earl Andrews recalls that they learned all they could from Stephen Ministries—which had pioneered in crisis ministry by laity, and was moving into training laity for regular pastoral care. Frazer later joined forces with International Lay Pastoring Ministry, whose prime mover is Melvin Steinbron, author of *Can the Pastor Do It Alone?*[10]

Frazer moved toward lay pastoral care in 1988 with the recognition that the redundant caring system already in place was not sufficient. They already had teams of laypeople providing hospital, nursing home, and shut-in visitation. They already had a staff of professional counselors. All new members had a sponsor, and several thousand other people were involved in Sunday school classes, small groups, support groups, and ministry groups in which care for one another (and often by a leader) was an intentional component. They also needed a volunteer staff of lay ministers who were gifted and trained for ministries of pastoral care.

They set a goal of providing a lay shepherd for every five family units in the church. Marie Parma, the staffer who now directs Frazer's lay ministers program, confesses that they have not yet achieved that goal. She adds that

> we may never cover all of our members this way, but that is okay, because we have a redundant caring system. Within our limitations, we *prioritize* the deployment of the 175 lay ministers we do have in place. We give priority to assigning a lay minister to new members, to members in crisis, to people who aren't in a Sunday School class, small group, or lay ministry, and to members who request a lay minister.

Frazer recruits, trains, and assigns new lay ministers twice a year. The training emphasizes Melvin Steinbron's prescription. "What does a lay pastor do? . . . We equip our lay pastors to do four things and to know that as they do these they are actually pastoring people." These four areas are easily remembered by the acrostic P.A.C.E.[11]

P—*P*ray for each one regularly.
A—Be *a*vailable.
C—*C*ontact each one on a regular basis.
E—Provide a Christian *example*.

Marie Parma speculated on why it is difficult to recruit enough lay ministers. "The 'E' may be a barrier; some people do not think of themselves as an actual example of what Jesus had in mind. Also, they think it is more time consuming than it really is."

Frazer has not yet found a way to produce enough lay ministers. Furthermore, Earl Andrews stresses that the management of a lay ministers program is even more "labor intensive" than most volunteer ministries. Yet they believe that lay ministries, including lay pastoral care, is the wave of the future and the indispensable key to the New Reformation that is possible in this emerging generation. Andrews reports that "we do see some other churches, now, bucking the clergy-driven church inertia to become lay-driven. Frazer is committed to helping many churches experience this crucial paradigm shift." They urge interested church leaders to connect with

Mel Steinbron
Pastoral Care Services
Hope Presbyterian Church
7132 Portland Avenue South
Minneapolis, MN 55423
(612) 866-4055

and to attend the organization's annual (April) "International Conference on the Pastoral Care of the Congregation by Lay People."

We have several reasons to raise up gifted laity to do lay pastoring. Christian people need regular pastoring, and the pastor cannot do it alone. Laity who do pastoring are blessed, and experience growth. Active lay pastors are more likely to commend the faith to people who do not follow Christ. Christians who engage in regular spiritual conversation with a pastor or spiritual director are also more likely to be contagious outreaching Christians.

The Rise of an Entrepreneurial Laity

The apostolic congregation continues where the traditional congregation leaves off. Both types of churches offer the "basic" ministries—worship, Christian education, and counseling; baptisms, weddings, and funerals, though we have seen that the apostolic congregation often does them differently—with different goals for people, with greater cultural relevance. Many traditional congregations offer little or nothing beyond the basic ministries, but apostolic congregations typically offer a wide range of ministries beyond the basics. Often, they are better known for their "special ministries" than for their "regular ministries." Their ministries, say, to singles, or the hearing impaired, or persons with addictions, or Vietnam veterans, or people with AIDS and their families, set them apart, define their public "image," and often achieve visibility for the church in the entire community.

Furthermore, most of an apostolic congregation's special ministries are the brainchildren of laypeople. In traditional congregations, the clergy generally define, and control, the church's entire agenda. Apostolic congregations, however, welcome and depend upon the ideas of laypeople for new ministries. Most of their new ministries were first conceived of in the imaginations of compassionate laypeople as, in their community traffic patterns, they perceived unmet needs. Every apostolic congregation I have studied has produced and/or attracted an entrepreneurial laity.

When a member of **Saddleback Valley Community Church** has a "hot idea" for a new ministry, the church observes the following procedure. The layperson presents the idea to Rick Warren, or someone else on the staff, who often responds by saying "Why not?" Even if a similar idea was tried before and failed, this may be the right time, or this might be the right person to pull it off. Warren explains that "if the idea seems screwball, it is better to let them find it out than for you to tell them. Why make me the bad guy? If you are the dream buster—telling people their idea won't fly—pretty soon your people quit trying!"

Often, Warren or another minister will respond by saying, "Great, you are it!" They presume that the person to whom God entrusted the idea is probably also the person to head the proposed ministry. The leaders announce the idea to the whole membership, and they call a meeting for all interested persons. If, after the meeting, enough people own the idea to make it fly, and if the leadership it would need is available, it becomes a new ministry of Saddleback Church. (No church "board" has to give permission!)

Saddleback Church policy states that any member may begin a new ministry as long as they follow four guidelines:

1. You don't expect the staff to run it.
2. You are in philosophical and doctrinal harmony with the church.
3. The ministry will not harm the testimony of the church.
4. You do not do any fund-raising.

(If a group needs money for a new ministry, they submit a cost estimate to the church for budget considerations. Rick Warren says, "If it is a ministry of the church, we will fund it in the budget. You can't have a unified church without a unified budget. And if you allow 75 different ministries to each do fund-raisers, you will kill your people with fund-raisers and alienate the seekers who have heard that churches are always asking for money.")

Much of the history of Saddleback Church is the history of the incarnation of laypeople's ideas into ministries. One member observed the mountains-to-desert range of opportunities available in Southern California's natural setting and conceived of a backpacking ministry as a means of both fellowship and evangelism; 75 people are now involved. Another member, a computer buff, formed a committee and started a Christian bulletin board service. Laypeople originally saw the need for what became Saddleback's Divorce Recovery Workshop, and for most of the church's other recovery ministries and support groups. Rick Warren has observed that "people will be as creative as you allow them to be. If your structure is simple enough for creativity to bubble up, your people's creativity will amaze you!"

The leaders of apostolic congregations often reinforce the core values that laity are called to be in ministry, and to create ministry. One day a woman fed a homeless person, paid for a night's lodging, and paid for a bus ticket back home. The next Sunday, she reported this to Rick Warren and exclaimed that "the church ought to do something about the homeless problem." Warren responded: "It sounds to me like the church did! Who is the church? Not the pastors! You are the church!" The next Sunday, Warren announced from the pulpit, "I authorize each one of you to feed and clothe the hungry. You don't have to ask me, just go ahead and do it. You are all ministers of Christ!"

Much of Frazer Memorial United Methodist Church's growth, strength, and achievement is attributable to its entrepreneurial laity.

Some laypersons dream of ways that, within their constraints, they can make a contribution. For example, a housebound woman lives fifty miles from the church but watches the service weekly on television. She asked to join, and to be in ministry; from her home, she writes a letter of affirmation and encouragement to every new member after they join the church. Her ministry motivates many new members to also get involved in a ministry. Another woman, afflicted with unusual shyness, writes caring letters to people who are hospitalized or shut in. Still another woman perceived a problem that she decided to solve; she sharpens the pencils in the church's pew racks after services each week.

Other laypersons see a need and help organize a team of laity to meet it. A member gathered data on the number of functionally illiterate adults in Montgomery. Twenty people responded to the announcement of a new ministry to teach adults to read, received training, and are now teaching adults, one-on-one, how to read. Another member imagined and shaped the Divorce Recovery seminar and support groups that now attract 120 people from metropolitan Montgomery every Tuesday evening. A layman read of the opportunity to plant churches behind the former "iron curtain"; a Frazer team is helping to plant a Methodist church in what was Czechoslovakia. A dentist in the church leads medical and dental teams into a rural part of Guatemala.

A Frazer laywoman, concerned for homeless people, started a "show box" program—in which volunteers pack toiletry items and a New Testament. A Christian Job Exchange, completely managed by Frazer volunteers, helps to arrange employment for several hundred people per year. A team of Frazer volunteers engages in telephone ministries with callers from the church's programs on the ACTS cable television network. A hospice nurse organized a team of Frazer volunteers who devote time to Hospice of Montgomery according to their gifts, abilities, and interests; some assist in clerical or administrative work, others give emotional and spiritual support to terminally ill patients, others support the patients' families.

Carol Taylor, a Frazer member and a certified animal trainer, wondered how her unusual competence could be used in ministry. She conceived of PAWS, an acronym for "Pets Are Working Saints." Today, dogs, cats, rabbits, and birds (and their owners) are trained for ministries to assist therapy, and teams of animals and owners are deployed in children's centers, rehabilitation centers, prisons, nursing homes, and other places. The ministry is in such demand that Frazer has to advertise for more pets (and owners) to train and use. Many people, in prisons and other institutions, who have never responded to visitors from churches do respond to the animals, and to the Christians who cared enough to bring the animals. A rabbit named Rodney has become especially popular at children's centers, while Sparkle (a pomeranian) and Elvis (a cockatiel) have been big hits in nursing homes. In one nursing home, a cat purred on the lap of a man with Alzheimer's disease. He said, "Hello, kitty cat!" This was the first he had spoken in years; Frazer's people have learned to thank God for small miracles as well as big ones. More recently, the PAWS ministry has provided cockatiels to serve as pets for women on death row at a prison for women. Each month, Frazer women bring food and supplies for the birds, and company, conversation, and Bible study guides for the inmates.

Ministries to Non-Christians

The ministry of apostolic congregations to people outside their church membership is one of their most distinguishing features. Traditional churches minister to the members, and their families, almost exclusively. Apostolic congregations are in ministry to many distinct populations in the entire surrounding community, and most of their external ministries are the brainchildren of an entrepreneurial laity.

For example, Sharon Amos became involved with the **Ginghamsburg United Methodist Church** when her daughter Kim started asking her, at six-thirty on Sunday mornings, to drive her to a mall where she could take a bus and ride 28 miles to Vandalia, Ohio, where a friend would meet her and drive her five miles to the Ginghamsburg church. Sharon, and her husband Wayne, had to see what was so special about this church. They were drawn into its vision and began teaching Sunday school and sponsoring youth mission work projects to Chicago, New York City, Pittsburgh, and Mexico. In time, Sharon and Wayne developed "DreamBuilders," a summer youth work camp project in Dayton, rehabilitating housing for low-income families.

Pastor Mike Slaughter frees and admonishes his people to perceive, approach, and obey the messages and visions from "burning bushes." A laywoman dreamed of starting a women's ministry in her neighborhood and she organized it from scratch. A layman developed a children's ministry, and a preschool. The church's youth director dreamed of starting after-school clubhouses for inner-city Dayton children and youth; Ginghamsburg church's youth serve as the volunteer staff for three clubhouses. Ginghamsburg people have staffed The Clothesline, a clothing resale store, for more than a decade. Volunteers developed, and continue to staff, a food pantry and a furniture warehouse. Through the New Creation Care Center, thirty-five volunteers trained in the Stephen Ministries counsel and manage support groups with people in pain. Mike Slaughter believes that "it is the business of the church to help people identify God's burning bushes. Then we must throw gasoline, not water, on their burning bush."[12]

Many of the new ministries of apostolic congregations become doors for reaching people through what Southern Baptist executive Ron Johnson has called "Ministry Based Evangelism." Often, they reach people who were unreachable by the traditional evangelism of traditional churches that seems to assume that pre-Christian people are little more than "souls with ears." Through ministries that meet needs, you establish credibility, rapport, and responsiveness with people who would resist or ignore words without deeds.

A Frazer constellation of ministries serves as a case in point. A layperson suggested the need for a support group for expectant couples who have learned that their child might be handicapped in some way. In time, that led to another support group for parents with children with handicaps. One Friday evening per month, Frazer staffs its nursery for "Parents Night Out" for parents of children with handicaps. In time, they added Sunday nurseries for these children, and several Sunday school classes, and a couple of Sunday school classes for their parents, and even a support group for siblings of children with handicaps. These and several other related ministries were all conceived, developed, and staffed by laity and, under the overall theme "Frazer's Friends for Life," the ministries have attracted many families having children with handicaps into faith and fellowship.

This important connection between community ministries and reaching new people is a point at which some have criticized apostolic congregations without mercy. Some "critics" have accused the churches who minister to people's needs beyond their membership of "constantly scanning" their communities for "people in pain" whom the church can "exploit" in its "obsession" for "ever inflated church membership statistics."

What reasonable response can we make to that charge? It *is* possible to find ministers like that, just as one can find ambulance-chasing lawyers, publicity-seeking professors, and quick-surgery physicians, in most any city. No profession is completely protected from practitioners with low motives. (Indeed, we have no reason to believe that professional "critics" are driven by motives as pure as the driven snow!)

However, to the critics' insinuation that growing congregations with community ministries are exploiters, four comments come to mind. First, ministry based evangelism is more biblical, that is, closer to what Jesus and the early apostles did than evangelism alone. Second, some of these same writers have criticized churches who do evangelism only—without also ministering to the needs of people in the community! (Some "critics" have it both ways!) Third, some of us believe that evangelism is so important that, if we did everything else for people except teach the gospel, invite them to follow Christ through his Church, and deploy them in the movement—we would leave them ultimately impoverished, and we would be guilty of the "paternalism" for which the same critics have often accused the Christian mission in other cultures. (Some critics have it all three ways!)

Fourth, while many community ministries do result in new members, many do not. For example, how many new members has Frazer likely received from death row, or the nursing homes, or the homeless population, or the hospice patient population? We could expand this list. For instance, Frazer has a van and a volunteer staff who are on call at any time, like the old volunteer fire departments, for disaster relief ministries. They are equipped and trained to help victims of hurricanes, tornadoes, floods, and so on. So far, every person this ministry has ever helped has lived too far away to become a Frazer member. The critics of such churches, who claim their only agenda is ministerial ambition and statistical church growth, have consistently taken the precaution of avoiding many facts!

Many of the ministries of apostolic congregations do not yield many new members, though there are exceptions. For 22 years Frazer people have been involved in prison ministry, from which they have received at least one new member. Tommy Waites was serving a life sentence when some men from Frazer befriended him. In time, he believed, started following

Christ, and experienced life change. When he came up for parole consideration, several Frazer men helped win his parole. He joined Frazer church, came to work on the church's custodial staff, and later pastored a Frazer-sponsored mission project—Bell Street Church.

Vineyard Community Church of Cincinnati has pioneered a distinctive approach to community ministry and evangelism. Their many expressions of "Servant Evangelism" in greater Cincinnati have given the church remarkable visibility and a positive image, and many people every week are motivated to "check it out." For example, teams of volunteers gift wrap packages at a mall every Christmas season as a ministry, for which donations are not accepted. They have been known to give away soft drinks at Bengal football games, to clean the toilets in bars and gas stations, wash cars, clean windshields, feed parking meters, give Gatorade to joggers and bikers, to rake leaves, mow lawns, clean gutters, shovel snow, and engage in many other spontaneous service projects. They accept no donations, and often utter only one sentence: "We just want to show you God's love in a practical way." Pastor Steve Sjogren defines servant evangelism as "Demonstrating the kindness of God by offering to do some humble act of service with no strings attached."[13] Sjogren believes that the gospel must be both spoken and shown in the secular world today. He believes that servant evangelism is the "low risk, high grace" approach that can involve more people than other approaches to evangelism.[14] He and his people have noticed that five discoveries especially empower service evangelism:[15]

1. People listen when I treat them like friends.
2. When I serve, hearts are touched.
3. As I serve, I redefine the perception of a Christian.
4. Doing the message precedes telling the message.
5. Focus on planting, not harvesting.

Willow Creek Community Church has discovered a trend in recent years that led them to another significant innovation in lay ministry. The church's leaders discovered that many people no longer come to a church struggling with a single problem. For instance, the same woman may have a food addiction, and be unemployed, experiencing financial difficulty, with a kid in trouble, and estranged from her husband. In response, Willow Creek has developed a cadre of 50 to 60 volunteer *case workers* whose lay ministry is to interview people to assess their multiple needs, and to work with them to develop a comprehensive plan to meet their needs.

Will Traditional Churches
Release Their Laity in Ministry?

When lay ministry gets as sophisticated as Willow Creek's deployment of lay case workers, we glimpse the unlimited possibilities for grassroots Christian lay movements, and we are shaken by the extent of the paradigm shift that traditional church leaders must experience before their churches will ever move from tradition to mission. The possibilities of most churches are frustrated more by the clergy's limited view of the faith, vision, and giftedness of the laity than by any other single factor.

For the apostolic renewal of our churches to happen while most of us yet live, many clergy (and denominational leaders) would need to experience a major paradigm shift related to John Wesley's alleged problem of seeing too many of his "geese" as "swans." That is not our problem. Too many of us see our swans as geese, and our geese as chickens or turkeys—or as mere geese who lay the golden eggs that fund the ecclesiastical machinery. Since no one sees people exactly as they are, Mr. Wesley erred on the better side. If we choose to see our people as gifted and shaped for ministry and mission, some of them will let God down; but many will become salt and light, and our churches will become contagious movements again.

So this chapter concludes by raising two questions in clear relief. First, will our people ever rise off their pews and share their faith with people who have not yet experienced it? In my observation and interview research, the correlation between lay ministry and witness is very high, perhaps the highest of any of the correlations I have emphasized in this book, even higher than whether Christians have had evangelism training. People who are involved in some ministry, for which they are gifted, who sometimes experience God working through their ministry or see fruits from their ministry, are enormously more likely than mere pew sitters to share their faith and invite people to involvement in the church. In my interviews with converts in churches, I always ask them who served as their "bridge" into the Possibility. In some churches, virtually all of the people doing any effective inviting beyond their own family are involved in some ministry. So, the issue of whether traditional churches will deploy their laity in ministry is also the issue of whether or not their people will ever function in apostolic ministry. The world needs churches whose laity minister and evangelize more than ever before.

Second, will our people ever experience the power and the fulfillment that comes only from experiencing the action and making a contribution in the lives of people, and is never experienced sitting on the sidelines? To be sure, the people in our traditional churches are part of the problem. They

145

are no more immune from sloth than the clergy, and they are accomplices to the clergy-laity heresy; they misperceive themselves as second-class citizens of the Kingdom, and few experiences in their church have suggested their giftedness or what difference makers they could be. We owe it to our loyal parishioners to help them discover their gifts, and discover a ministry, and experience the growth and fulfillment that comes only from involvement in ministry.

Ginger Scott, a young nurse by profession and a member of Frazer Church, became a lay minister. She took the training and met the families assigned to her. The more she prayed for and with them, was available to them, regularly contacted them, and tried to serve as an example, the more meaningful it became. One of "her" people was Margie, a woman in her early sixties whose husband had died. Margie once had cancer; it now returned and, after several months of pain and struggle, she died. Throughout that experience, Ginger contacted her, supported her, and reminded her of the Promises and of Who was suffering with her. Margie died in October, 1990. Months later, Ginger wrote this letter to Margie Parma, director of the Lay Ministers program at Frazer:

Dear Marie:

Over the last few days I have spent a lot of time thinking about Margie. She was such a special lady. I thought back to when you first asked me to consider being her lay minister and I had to really pray about it because I didn't know if I could do another person. But the details you had shared with me, that she was a recent widow and had cancer herself, made me think I would probably be real comfortable spending time with her. Little did I know I would be so Blessed.

Margie let me love her. This meant so much. It's amazing to me how God's love can bind two strangers in such a short time. Margie would share her heart with me (her sadness, her hopes, dreams, fears, even her love stories!). Sometimes she would call and say "I just wanted to tell you" or "can you talk?" On one occasion I remember I dropped by her house with a surprise for her, and when she opened up the door she began to cry, and said "You don't know how much I need you right now and how I talked myself out of calling you."

There were many times when she was hospitalized that she would let me crawl up in that bed and just hold her—we'd cry, laugh, talk, and pray. But she let me love her.

She'll never know how much I needed to love her. It had been years since I've been able to love without fear of rejection—but I always knew Margie would love me back.

Marie, thank you for asking me to be her lay minister because as a result, I got "love with skin on it."

I love you,

Ginger Scott

Since Ginger Scott received the strength to face the risks in love, she has married, and is now Ginger Scott Pearson. She moved with her husband near Huntsville, Alabama. She is still in lay ministry, but she has shifted her vocation. Ginger is now a hospice nurse, devoting her life to terminally ill people. Except for the details, her story is not unique.

When you lose your life in Kingdom ministry, you join the active ranks of "the salt of the earth" and "the light of the world," and over time you find your life and you discover yourself being saved and made whole. Doesn't every Christian have the inalienable right to the kinds of experiences in which Christianity can deliver on its greatest promises?

CHAPTER SIX

✠

How Apostolic Churches Reach Secular People

Like an increasing number of people in our communities, Ginny Wheeler was raised in a family that did not profess faith and never went to church. Ginny experienced some interest in faith and church, and occasionally attended Sunday school with a neighbor, "But I just didn't feel like I belonged." She grew up, graduated from college, became a public school teacher, married Lee, and had her first child, Katy, eleven years later.

When Ginny decided to place Katy in a preschool, she reports, "I interviewed preschools like most people interview colleges" and they placed Katy in a Lutheran preschool. "Then," Ginny reports, "our little girl came home asking questions I couldn't answer. She asked why didn't we go to Sunday school, so she would have something to say during sharing time." Ginny and Lee moved finding a church to the top of their list, and "shopped" for a Lutheran church—to be consistent with the preschool.

One Sunday in 1981, Ginny, Lee, and their two children visited The Community Church of Joy. "First time in the door, I felt so welcomed and so loved, and I couldn't believe church could be this much fun! I was just visiting the church out of duty, but I loved it and I couldn't wait to come back. . . . I now know God directed me here, because many Lutheran churches might not have been as accepting or made me feel as comfortable." They joined the church—even though Lee, also raised unchurched, "was still kind of kicking and screaming!" In time, he became president of the church council, and Ginny became the staff director for adult education.

Soon after joining, Ginny volunteered to teach Sunday school. The church sent her to a denominational training event in Tempe, Arizona for 450 new Sunday school teachers. She carried a small white King James Bible that a Baptist Sunday school class had given her when she once visited as a second grader. When the leader asked participants to turn to 3 John 3:12, Ginny drew a blank. "I vaguely remembered Matthew, Mark, Luke, and John, but this Third John was news to me!" In part to avoid future embarrassments, she undertook a year-long overview of the Bible. "Gradually, I developed a passion for the Bible. I fell in love with the Book. I had thought that only pastors could interpret it. Then I realized it was a road map for my life." In time, Ginny developed the church's *Discover the Bible* curriculum that roots many other people in the scriptures.

One day, Ginny was sharing the meaning of her new faith with her cousin Janet and her husband Don. She invited them to visit the Community Church of Joy. "Don had never been in a church, ever" but they and their two children came and are involved disciples today. Ginny learned to relate to other parents at kids' soccer games and Girl Scouts, and from those friendships "Lee Ann and Tom and their three children are here."

Ginny became friends with Katy's first grade teacher—Laurie. Her husband Doug had never been in a church except the day they married. "It took awhile," but Laurie, Doug, and their two children became followers of Jesus through the Community Church of Joy. In time Laurie brought her parents, George and Gloria, into the church, and Laurie's sister Debbie, her husband, and their three children all became members.

Ginny joined the PTA and, in time, the president and vice-president each visited the Community Church of Joy and joined, each with her husband and three children. Lee has brought several colleagues from his office into the church. Their girls have already served as "bridges" on several occasions. Ginny explains: "When a girl spends Saturday night with our girls, the invitation includes church the next morning. Several girls have gone home saying 'Church was fun! Dad, you ought to go'—and have joined, with their parents and siblings."

For three years, as Ginny visited her dentist's office each December, she gave a Christmas service brochure to the dental hygienist. "She was unchurched and nervous, but each time she would ask me questions." In December of 1992, the dental hygienist, her husband, and their two children attended a Christmas service. They began attending, took some classes, made some friends, discovered faith, and joined the church. One Sunday, Ginny reports, "They were serving communion, and it just brought tears to my eyes."

Ginny Wheeler reports these experiences in the church's fourth seminar for new members, and then suggests:

> So I want to encourage you. You don't have to be pushy. Your example, your encouragement, and your welcome are going to bring lots of people here. This is just to show you that you can go out, and without having to quote scripture, or hit people over the head, or ring strange door bells—you are all evangelists! It is so exciting! The exciting part is to see lives changed.

People are usually very generous about thanking you for bringing them here, so it's not something you need to be embarrassed about or apologize for. You need to start looking for the opportunities, as they show up, to invite people. I guarantee you, coming from that background myself, many people are just waiting for an invitation. The more they like you, the more they are going to accept that invitation. So, think of yourselves as evangelists, because that is really how this church has grown as large as it is.

Called, Sent, and Culturally Relevant . . .

The first five chapters delineated the distinctive shape of the "apostolic congregation" that reaches unchurched pre-Christian people, and produces contagious Christians, like Ginny and Lee Wheeler. This type of congregation, which has come to the surface in history before, was "born again" in North America in the 1970s.

These churches are "apostolic," in part, because their leaders are convinced that they are "called" and "sent" to reach an undiscipled population. For instance, Rick Warren planted Saddleback Valley Community Church precisely to reach the educated, affluent, laid-back but stressed-out pagan population of Orange County, California. Dale Galloway planted New Hope Community Church in Portland to bring "new hope" to struggling, dysfunctional, working-class people in Portland. John Ed Mathison perceived that there were more unreached people in the Deep South Bible Belt city of Montgomery than anyone imagined, so he moved to staid old Frazer Memorial United Methodist Church, planning to use the church's pending relocation to catalyze the church into mission. As Win Arn once featured in his film *And They Said It Couldn't Be Done*, Tom Wolf took leadership of The Church on Brady—believing God's promise that such a church could reach the struggling ethnic populations of East Los Angeles.

In October of 1984, Dieter Zander experienced an actual vision. "I have not had another one before or since. I was driving my car, after a soccer practice in Clarement, thinking about all the young people who were not attending any church. Tina Turner was singing 'What's Love Got to Do with It?' on the radio. Suddenly God dropped this vision into me." Zander envisioned a stage, with a band, drums, theater lighting, drama, and a high school gym full of faithful young people praising God. The vision impelled Dieter Zander to start New Song church in 1986—to reach the population that became known as "Baby Busters."

So these churches are "apostolic" in the sense, from the New Testament Greek *apostello*, that they are "sent out" by God to reach one or more distinct populations. They are also apostolic in the sense we featured in chapter 3: Like the early apostles and their communities, they adapt to the language, music, style, and forms of their target population's culture. Furthermore, their theology and message center upon the gospel of early apostolic Christianity.

Moreover, I suggested that the apostolic congregation represents a form of church life that Christianity often takes. Today's apostolic congregations are remarkably similar, in certain key features, to the early churches reflected in the New Testament, and to the Anabaptist, Pietist, and Methodist apostolic movements within Reformation Christianity. (I featured only the eighteenth-century Methodist precedent because I know it best, and because I needed to show some historical precedence for these congregations without making this a historical treatise.) The ten top features of apostolic congregations are also prominent in many growing Third World congregations today. (I was tempted to demonstrate this from apostolic Korean churches, but decided to confine the focus to mission in the secular West, particularly North America.)

. . . To Reach People

I also suggested that the Apostolic Congregation's main business is to communicate the Christian faith to the growing numbers of people who do not yet believe or follow Christ, including many who lack even a Christian memory. This agenda contrasts with the traditional congregation's main business of nurturing and caring for its members and their children. The apostolic congregation is essentially a "church for the unchurched," communicating the gospel to pre-Christian people. In a remarkable paradox however, the Church that best prepares people to reach out is also the best church to receive new people, nurture their growth, and send them out!

Once, we suggested, the challenge of communicating Christianity's message and worldview was not as formidable as it is today. In Christendom, the Church enjoyed a "home field advantage" in which the whole Western world marched to medieval Christianity's drum and played the game of life by the Church's rules; in that period the Church played a central role in Western society and influenced the worldview of virtually every citizen. Today, however, the West has been substantially secularized, and our society's many subcultures now march to a cacophony of competing drums. In this more secular world, an increasing number of people have lived their lives beyond the influence of any church, and they have no background for even knowing what Christians are talking about.

So, how do we reach the growing numbers of "secular people" in Western society, including the U.S.A.? On this question, the apostolic congregations have engaged in important pioneering on behalf of all churches. (The case of Ginny Wheeler illustrates several of the following principles.)

Ten Pioneering Principles of Outreach in Apostolic Churches

1. They prepare their people in multiple ways.

We have already devoted most of this book to developing one point: The apostolic church prepares its people for witness and invitation by rooting them in scripture, deepening them in prayer, teaching them compassion for sinners and obedience to the Great Commission, and by scripting them with an apostolic vision of what people can become. The apostolic church further prepares the way for outreach by involving its people in pastoral care, small groups, and lay ministries, and by offering many ministries to pre-Christian people—including a celebrative culturally relevant worship service that eliminates "the cringe factor" and frees Christians to invite their friends. Indeed, the Seeker Service, and the range of other ministries to pre-Christian people, are the apostolic church's replacements for the Sunday evening service, the revival, and the other inherited approaches that no longer engage non-Christians in significant numbers.

2. They clarify the goal of outreach.

Apostolic churches are clear that the goal of the gospel's communication is not merely to persuade people to believe, accept Christ's benefits, and join the ranks of nominal Christians. Many traditional churches are content with mere belief, membership, and attendance, but apostolic churches are not. In the words of Willow Creek's mission statement, the goal is "to turn irreligious people into fully devoted followers of Jesus Christ." (Chapter 3 expanded this goal into a comprehensive profile of the Christian which we join with the Spirit in making.)

Nominal Christianity does not meet the deep needs of people's souls. It cannot deliver on Christianity's great promises. Seekers do not detect "the authentic sign" from nominal Christians. Apostolic congregations view their mission fields as John Wesley once faced a nation of mere nominal Christians in eighteenth-century England; he regarded England as, for all practical purposes, "a pagan land." He observed, in his essay "The Doctrine of Original Sin," that most of the English people were "brutishly ignorant" of the Christian faith and there was no evidence of their serious practice of that faith. He regarded his nation's nominal Christians as not "one jot above the pitch of a Turk or a Heathen."

From the pulpit of St. Mary's church in Oxford, Wesley exposed "Christian England" as a myth—in the sense that "Scriptural Christianity" was not to be substantially found in England, certainly not in Oxford, nor even in Oxford's leaders! David Bosch rightly concludes that Wesley and eighteenth-century Methodists "could see no real difference between nominal Christians and pagans and could not, by implication, distinguish between 'home' and 'foreign' missions. . . . The whole world was a mission field."[1] So, the apostolic mission still targets nominal Christians who are not fully devoted to the Kingdom.

3. They understand evangelism as a process.

The leaders of most apostolic churches are aware that making Christians necessarily involves a process, which takes place *in stages, over time*. Like the Hollywood myth that people "fall in love at first sight," many traditional churches assume that "instant" evangelism is possible, or ought to be; so one sermon, or lesson, or conversation, or visit to the church should be "enough" for seekers to decide whether to join or not. But apostolic congregations know that helping someone become a follower of Christ involves a more prolonged process—weeks, months, or years (usually months), so any one-shot "hypodermic" approach to evangelization is unrealistic, and likely counterproductive.

John Wesley understood a process approach to evangelism with great clarity. His model of the "Order of Salvation" involved four stages:

1. Lost people were first *awakened*—to their lost state, their sins, their need for God, to a desire to experience the grace of God.

2. Awakened people were *enrolled* in a Methodist class and, if persistent in their quest, into a Methodist society.

3. In time, awakened Methodists were *justified*, that is, they experienced God's acceptance.

4. In time, some justified Methodists were *sanctified*, that is, they experienced the completion, in this life, of the gracious work God began in their justification, and were now freed and empowered to live by God's will and by love for their neighbors.[2]

Studies of autobiographical accounts of eighteenth-century Methodists indicate that the gap in time between people's awakening and their experience of justification *averaged* about two years. Most Methodists never experienced their sanctification, but Wesley taught them that if they *expected* to be made, in this life, all they were meant to be, then they would live effective Christian lives. For early Methodism, then, a process led toward the goal of full devotion.

New Song Church teaches their people an imaginative process model:

The Stairway to
"Fully Devoted Followership"
New Song Church

Pre-Christian
Potential Christian
New Christian
Growing Christian
Reproducing Christian
Fully Devoted Christian
Extending Christian

The New Song model attempts to show that "growing into the likeness of Jesus Christ is 'Downward Mobility.'" The church accepts the responsibility of providing relevant ministries to people at each stage. The model helps Christians: (1) To perceive where people are in the process, (2) To identify ministries, training, resources, or experiences that might help people to move to the next stage, and (3) To know, therefore, how to refer people to specific ministries, training, resources, or experiences.

Willow Creek's leaders also define evangelism in terms of process. Their philosophy of evangelism claims that

> all people matter to God, and therefore to us. Yet, without a personal relationship with Christ, each of us would be eternally separated from God. People must be reached with the message of the gospel and given an opportunity to receive answers to their questions and objections. This must be done by us in a culturally relevant way, while recognizing that it generally takes unbelievers a period of time to go through the process of coming to the point of trusting Christ.[3]

Willow Creek's Impact Evangelism seminar emphasizes that, in the ministry of evangelism, we are catalyzing and facilitating a process. They assure their people that "you are just part of the process God is orchestrating in the person's life. He orchestrates other events too." They quote lines from Cliffe Knechtle's *Give Me An Answer:*

> A person's coming to Christ is like a chain with many links. There is the first link, middle links, and a last link. There are many influences and conversations that precede a person's decision to convert to Christ. I know the joy of being the first link at times, a middle link usually and occasionally the last link. God has not called me to only be the last link. He has called me to be faithful and to love all people.[4]

155

Willow Creek alerts its people to the fact that "you won't be the whole chain." They affirm that every link in the chain is as important as the last link. "It does not matter who seals the deal. Be the link, or links, God calls you to be with this person."

Willow Creek's version of a process model involves nine components:

Stages of Spiritual Growth

		*				*	*	*
Hostile to Spiritual Things	*Open Reproduc- tion to Spiritual Things*	*Seeking Actively Investi- gating Spiritual Things*	*Commit- ment*	*Learning about Jesus Christ & Christian Life*	*Changing Lifestyle Inner Change, New Priorities*	*Sm.Gp. Service Steward- ship*	*Christ- ian Life*

Willow Creek's leaders teach this model in the Impact Evangelism seminar and also teach it, annually, to all the members attending the New Community services that week. They use the model to remind people of the goal of evangelism—which is not getting one more conversion, but bringing people to full devotion to Jesus Christ. They also use the model to teach Christians the process they are cooperating with. "In most cases, your objective is to move them one step." The asterisks (*), incidentally, flag the zones between steps where people are most likely to "coast" and, therefore, where an intervention is often warranted.

Willow Creek's model helps us to see that we are working with a complex process, in which one encounters a mystery transcending any model or theory. From many cases, we know that the process does not move in a neat sequence. For example, some people learn quite a bit about Jesus Christ and the Christian life before they commit. Some people become, say, active in a small group earlier than the model would indicate and into (serious) stewardship later. The model also helps us understand why reality is more complex than this, or any, model. In given cases it may take several conversations, interventions, experiences, or ministries—over time—to move someone, say, from hostility into openness, with probably some reinforcement needed to keep them open long enough to move into active seeking.

4. They regard outreach as a lay ministry.

Traditional congregations assign outreach to the pastor, but apostolic congregations assign it to a prepared apostolic laity. In *How to Reach Secular People,* I submitted three reasons accounting for the lay approach's much greater effectiveness:

156

1. The laity have a better opportunity than the clergy to reach many pre-Christian people because they have many more contacts with the target population.

2. In evangelism, the "amateurs" outperform the "professionals," about two to one. There may be several factors accounting for this, but one factor is the ordained person's loss of credibility with about half of the unchurched population; the clergy are perceived as "paid" to commend the Christian religion and to recruit members for the institutional church.

3. Even when pastors succeed in recruiting new members, they often fail in the long run. Psychologically, the new members have "joined the pastor" more than really joining the church. So when that pastor leaves, retires, or dies, those members become inactive members in much greater numbers than the members who joined the church psychologically.[5]

As evangelical folk wisdom sometimes expresses it, "Shepherds do not make new sheep; sheep make new sheep." In an apostolic congregation, the people are clear that the church's main business is to serve, reach, and disciple people who do not yet understand, believe, or follow Christ as Lord. As all laity are called and gifted to be in ministry, so all Christians are called to the ministry of witness and invitation, and laity with the spiritual gift for evangelism are called to make it their main ministry.

5. They train their people for outreach.

We have emphasized the main ways in which apostolic churches prepare their people for outreach. We have observed that, in more and more communities, merely training the members of a traditional church for evangelism, without changing the church, is no longer productive. However, most members of an apostolic church are not sufficiently prepared without specific evangelism training. (Evangelism training is a necessary, but insufficient by itself, condition for producing an apostolic people.) Willow Creek's Impact Evangelism Seminar serves as an exemplar of the kind of training that is possible. The four sessions, two hours each, cover four important themes:

1. Being Yourself
2. Telling Your Story
3. Making the Message Clear
4. Communicating Effectively

6. They practice social network evangelism.

As Ginny Wheeler and her converts engaged friends and relatives with the Christian possibility in an expanding "web of influence," so all apostolic congregations encourage and teach social network evangelism as the way in which the faith spreads "naturally." Church growth research has demonstrated that whenever and wherever the Christian faith has spread, it has spread along social networks. The leaders of apostolic churches know this (and the other basic insights of church growth lore), and the insight is repeatedly confirmed in their church's outreach experience. The Christian faith spreads among secular Western populations like it spreads among other populations—across "the bridges of God" (Donald A. McGavran) provided by the kinship and friendship networks of believers, especially new believers. Most converts out of secularity report that the good news, and the opportunity to follow Christ, were communicated to them by a trusted friend, neighbor, colleague, or relative. They often report that one to several other Christians, or a group of Christians or seekers, also play a role in their evangelization. Paul still plants, and Apollos still waters. All the apostolic churches in this study teach and advocate outreach across social networks.

Tom Wolf, of the Church on Brady, emphasizes reaching "households" and then spreading the faith within them. Wolf, with many New Testament scholars and missiologists, perceives strategic significance in the Greek New Testament term *oikos* which is usually translated "household." Luke tells us (Acts 10:2) that Cornelius "feared God with all his [*oikos*]," and Paul tells the Philippian jailer (Acts 16:31) to "Believe on the Lord Jesus Christ and you will be saved, you and your [*oikos*]."

The *oikos* (household) was the basic unit of Greco-Roman society, but it reached more widely than today's nuclear family; one's *oikos* could include one's clients, friends, and kinsmen, and even one's slaves, as well as one's spouse and blood relations. This social unit was essentially relational, that is, all the people who actually lived and related within this social unit were de facto members of a given "household." The early church spread naturally within the given household, and between households that were somewhat connected to each other.

Tom Wolf believes that

> *oikos* Evangelism is normative, New Testament evangelism. It is the God-given and God-ordained means for naturally sharing the supernatural message. It transcends cultures and is relevant to the struggles of any generation. . . . It is sharing the astoundingly good news about Jesus in one's own sphere of influence, the interlocking social systems composed of family, friends, and associates.[6]

He believes that the *oikos* principle is the way forward in the cities of the earth, and that it yields the greatest life transformation. With this strategy, churches can experience something like the spontaneous expansion of early Christianity; without it, urban churches will continue feeling overwhelmed by the mandate to evangelize their communities.

All the apostolic churches of this study advocate social network outreach. Between 75 and 90 percent of all their new members were connected to a Christian in their kinship or friendship network who served as their bridge into the faith.

At least two of the churches, Willow Creek and Community Church of Joy, would add one point. In today's very large secular cities, a growing number of pre-Christian people are not already linked, by friendship or kinship, to any living Christian from whom they are likely to receive the possibility. In such a secular context, our mandate backs up one step. Often, before we can invite a friend we have to make a friend. So, the first step in Willow Creek's Seven Step Strategy calls for a Christian to "befriend Unchurched Harry."

7. They offer "the faith once delivered to the saints."

Apostolic churches believe that all we have to offer the human race is original Christianity, "the faith once delivered to the saints." In this sense, apostolic churches are rooted within theological orthodoxy, and so have *much* more in common with traditional evangelical churches than with churches who accept all religious points of view as more or less equally valid. Apostolic churches substantially concur with traditional evangelical churches regarding the *content* of the Christian message, though they are not as confident that the nineteenth-century leaders got the message exactly right, nor that their favored themes should necessarily be ours. Apostolic churches are profoundly influenced by their tradition, but their primary source is the Bible, and their mission is to meaningfully communicate the biblical message to the pre-Christian people of their generation.

Consequently, apostolic congregations pay the price to understand their target population, and they take them seriously. They have observed that the pre-Christians who become receptive to Christianity want "the real thing." There is virtually no market, among secular people, for new theologies or alleged "improvements" upon original Christianity. Pre-Christians who prefer something "new" do not often move toward some new version of Christianity; they gravitate toward some non-Christian religious option now available in the religious marketplace. Those who turn to Christianity want to be in touch with the same meaning and reality that Christianity has represented, with *some* consistency, since earliest times.

In part because apostolic churches begin where the people are that they are called to reach, they do not share the traditional evangelical's interest in dogma, nor even in theological controversy about doctrines that are not central to Christianity. The target populations do ask important theological questions, but not the same questions that interest most academic theologians. For example, New Hope Community Church had a weekly call-in radio program in the mid-1980s. In one 49-week period in 1985, they received and coded 5,122 telephone inquiries. They received fewer questions on doctrinal issues than those in any other category. There were far more questions about illness, stress, finances, marriage, children, making sense of life, and so on. New Hope's associate pastor David Durey tells pastors: "They are not interested in your doctrinal distinctive or mine."

8. They address the "life concerns" of pre-Christians (and Christians).

Sometimes, traditional evangelical churches do not perceive their kinship with apostolic churches, because the latter do not confine their preaching and teaching to the traditional evangelical themes. They are as likely to address human struggles like anxiety, or self-esteem, or out-of-control feelings as they are to preach on the forgiveness of sins, or justification by faith, or life after death. This wider agenda may confuse traditional evangelical leaders, but is sufficiently explained by Paul Hiebert's influential essay "The Flaw of the Excluded Middle."[7]

Hiebert explains that people in most nonwestern societies include three "levels" (low, middle, and high) in their worldview. The *lower level* is the "real," "natural," or "material" world available to the senses. The *middle level* is an immanent spiritual realm that affects people's crops, business, health, fertility, child rearing, family relations, social relations, and other immediate concerns of their daily lives. The middle level, Hiebert reports, focuses on "the uncertainties of the future; the crises of the present; and the unexplainable events of the past. The meaning of human experiences."[8] The *high level* is the transcendent spiritual level in which people focus on cosmic issues like "the ultimate story of the origin, purpose and destiny of the self, society and universe."[9]

Hiebert then offers three explanations that illuminate many matters for the Christian mission in the West: (1) The "high religions," like Christianity, Hinduism, Buddhism, and Islam, tend to confine their focus to the higher level, the cosmic issues. Thus they ignore the middle level, abdicating it to Shamans, Witch Doctors, Astrologers, and other practitioners of folk religions. (2) The Western world (especially Western intellectuals), influenced by the Enlightenment, focuses largely on the lower empirical world available to the senses, while excluding the middle from its worldview (and, I would add, regarding the higher level as "optional"). In any case, "The most important feature of this Enlightenment worldview is that the spiritual and real worlds do not touch. We have been taught to believe they are wholly separate."[10] (3) Hiebert observes that many missionaries, operating from their Western worldview, have missed many peoples by ministering only at the low level and the high level, ignoring their middle-level concerns; consequently, even their converts are forced to revert to pre-Christian practices to cope with ordinary life concerns. By contrast, Hiebert reports, "It is no coincidence that many of the most successful missions have provided some form of Christian answer to middle level questions."[11]

As New Hope Community Church's call-in radio program revealed, middle level questions now drive ordinary people in the West more than higher level issues. We observe, furthermore, that if Christian churches do not address these questions meaningfully, the people (pre-Christians *and* some of our Christians) will turn to some astrologer, therapist, newspaper columnist, or guru, or to their peer group or cultural values or favorite soap opera, who will address them.

Traditional churches largely confine their focus and themes to the ultimate or higher theological matters (though prayer for the sick is one widespread exception). Apostolic churches, however, are learning to address the middle level as well as the higher level (and some are also helping their people to see how God is involved in the lower level as well). I suggest that the traditional church's preoccupation with the higher level reflects the (unconscious) influence of the Enlightenment. I suggest that Apostolic churches have clear biblical warrant for ministering within the middle level, and for beginning with the seeker's felt needs and driving questions. So, for good reason, apostolic pastors like Dale Galloway write books for seekers like *The Fine Art of Getting Along with Others, The Awesome Power of Your Attitudes, Dare to Discipline Yourself*, and *Rebuild Your Life*. The public hunger for Christianity to engage people's middle level questions explains the wide circulation of David Seamands' books, such as *The Healing of Memories* and *The Healing of Damaged Emotions*.

9. They use the language of the target population.

As apostolic churches often contrast with traditional evangelical churches in the themes they address, they also contrast with traditional evangelical churches in matters of form, and style, and especially *language*. Apostolic congregations in the English-speaking world know that the secular people who are open to Christianity do not, generally, respond to the faith if it is expressed in Elizabethan, academic, theological, evangelical, ecclesiastical, or "politically correct" language.

The gospel must be meaningfully interpreted in the people's language for them to comprehend and appropriate it. The late C. S. Lewis reminds us that we expect our missionaries to the Bantus to learn Bantu, but we never ask whether our missionaries to the Americans or the English can speak American or English. Lewis commented that any fool can prattle academic or ecclesiastical jargon. The test, he said, is communication "in the vernacular."

10. They represent the gospel with generational relevance.

In many mission fields of the earth, the culture changes some from one generation to the next. If the churches simply perpetuate the forms that the old people like, they risk missing a generation of non-Christians *and* losing the rising generation of Christians. Apostolic churches in North America have perceived this factor operating in American Christianity. They know that the Church's own young people share much of the contemporary culture with secular pagans, such as its music preferences.

Consequently, they have discovered that the same approaches that engage unchurched pre-Christians of the culture engage (and retain) many of their own youth and young adults; likewise, the church's young people can often identify the ways to reach unchurched pagans. The secular people and the churched youth who respond to Christianity do not, generally, respond to traditional church forms like robed choirs, or pipe organ music, or nineteenth-century hymns, or a "ministerial" tone from the pulpit. The same generation who will not buy their father's Oldsmobile will not buy a church whose language, inflection, music, and style are from their parents' generation. In this mission field, like all others, the church that engages outsiders and the rising generation is indigenous, that is, it expresses the faith's meaning through contemporary culturally relevant speech, music, liturgy, clothing, leadership style, and so on.

P.S.: They know that "God gives the increase."

While the apostolic congregations have pioneered distinct approaches to reaching unchurched pre-Christian people, they do not over rely on their discoveries. They keep rediscovering that Paul was right in his observation that "no one can say 'Jesus is Lord' except by the Holy Spirit." By his prevenient grace the Holy Spirit prepares us, and by his empowering grace he prepares and empowers us to be his ambassadors, through whom he will make his appeal. When, in our ministry to secular seekers, the penny drops and the bell rings and they discover the gift of faith, it is not primarily because of our great theology or sophisticated approach or communication skill, but because the Holy Spirit has broken through in revealing grace. Paul still plants, Apollos still waters, and God still gives the increase. So, apostolic churches know to depend on the Holy Spirit in the ministries of evangelism.

Ten Ways That Apostolic Churches Communicate the Gospel

My research with secular converts, Christian communicators, and apostolic churches has led me to ten more specific principles about the gospel's effective communication. Any would-be communicator of Christianity to secular people might keep the following points in mind.

1. They often begin with "active listening."

Russell Hale has often said that "most people can't hear until they have been heard," and "People don't care how much you know until they know how much you care." The "active" part of active listening involves giving people "feedback." Having heard them, we phrase in our words what we understood they meant *plus* our sense of how they felt. Tim Wright teaches the people of Community Church of Joy to listen especially to people's stories. Story-listening conveys unconditional love and empathy and helps Christians to infer their needs implied in their stories. Then, seekers will "listen best when the message applies to a need within their life."

2. They begin where the people are.

Donald Soper often declared that "we must begin where people are, rather than where we would like them to be." This strategy often involves the demonstration of Christianity's relevance—by "scratching where people itch," by engaging their felt needs. Often, converts out of secularity report that Christ first helped them by raising their sense of dignity and self-worth, or by giving them power over some problem (such as an addiction) around which life had become unmanageable.

Beginning with people's felt needs or driving motives is not necessarily the "pandering," that is, "just giving people what they want," that some critics have charged. We do offer the gospel as the fulfillment of some needs and wants that people have, such as their need for dignity. But we offer the gospel as God's liberating power from some other needs and wants—such as people's greed, or their quest to escape into the perfect "high." Furthermore, we know that people's felt needs are often symptoms of their deeper Need for forgiveness, justification, reconciliation, or the power of the Holy Spirit. The gospel addresses both the need and the Need; so should we.

3. They teach "Christianity 101" . . .

Churches often reach people through the ministry of basic instruction that Willow Creek has labeled "Christianity 101." Since, in a secular age, our target population no longer understands elementary Christianity, we begin where they are cognitively rather than where we would like them to be. Soper has long emphasized that any apostle, today, must be prepared to spend his or her whole life "explaining basic Christianity to people, what it basically teaches, claims, stands for, and offers—rather than what they take it to be."

We have learned two particularly important things about this ministry of instruction. First, we advance the clarity of our truth claims more through story and analogy than through theological abstractions and arguments. For instance, St. Patrick explained our Christian understanding of "One God in Three Persons" through the humble analogy of the Irish shamrock: while a shamrock is one plant, its three connected but distinct leaves suggest how the Father, the Son, and the Holy Spirit can be distinct expressions of the one God.

Second, we have learned in adult education about the need to get adults "involved" in their learning. This has led some churches to convene and work with "seeker groups " as follows: The group leader is more facilitator than teacher. As group members raise questions about, say, Christianity's understanding of God as a "Trinity," the facilitator lends two or three participants some resources from the church library and these participants do their homework and present this Christian teaching at the next meeting of the seekers group. Several apostolic churches now stock their church libraries (or book shops) with books, videos, and other materials with proven usefulness to secular seekers.

. . . 4. From a reduced canon.

With some secular people, though not quite a majority, we share from a functionally reduced biblical canon in our early conversations. Some secular people associate Paul's letters with the "dogmatism," and the Old Testament with the "legalism," that turns them off; but they are usually open to Jesus, and very interested in what Jesus taught, so our earliest witnessing may be from the gospels.

Which gospel is best to use with seekers? The experience-based wisdom circulating in several of the apostolic churches suggests using Luke's Gospel with most people; but using Matthew with Jewish people, John with philosophically oriented people, or Mark with people who are addicted, dysfunctional, or who struggle with other "power" problems.

5. They practice the "miracle of dialogue."

Many secular people who become believing Christians discover this possibility through what Reuel Howe called "the miracle of dialogue." The ministry of caring, intelligent conversation—especially conversation

164

around their questions and doubts—helps to open more secular people to the possibility of faith than any other single approach I know of.

Through experience with secular doubters and seekers, I have learned three things about the ministry of reasonable conversation (or "Apologetics") that are worth passing on: (1) You will discover that those years you have spent studying the scriptures and theology are a reproductive investment. You have already been entrusted with faithful satisfying answers to some of the questions that secular people ask!

(2) You will hear them asking some other questions for which you do not, for now, have sufficient answers. That discovery will drive you to your knees, to the scriptures, and to theological study and reflection, and—in reflecting upon questions you could not answer—you will learn more useful theology than you could in a degree program of "desk theology."

(3) They will ask some questions for which you will not have, and cannot find, answers they will find immediately satisfying, but that will not ultimately matter. They didn't need all of their questions answered, but only enough of them to know that Christianity is supported by good reasons. Besides, they never expected *you* to be an arch-guru with the answers to *all* of humanity's most perplexing questions.

From honest dialogue with you, they have now had the experience of several conversations with a nondefensive, nonjudgmental Christian who cared enough to be vulnerable and talk through their doubts with them, and that experience is often used by the Holy Spirit. You have given them enough good reasons for them to know that Christianity is a reasonable venture, and often they will bring their remaining doubts with them into the first steps of faith.

6. They cooperate with the principle of "cumulative effect."

In part because the Christian gospel is a multifaceted gem, no one "gets" the message from one exposure. It typically takes weeks or months to come to adequate terms with the gospel's meaning, its implications, and the costs of being a disciple. Because no one gets it the first time, the principle of "cumulative effect" instructs the Christian advocate. The seeker's repeated exposure to, say, the meaning of "grace" is necessary for most secular seekers to be able to adopt the faith.

7. They practice the principle of "creative redundancy."

The repeated communication of the same message over time, however, is not achieved by mere repetition, because that loses the receiver's attention and interest long before adoption can occur. So the companion principle is creative redundancy. The effective gospel communicator develops the capacity to say the same thing in a dozen or more different ways. The apostle Paul models this principle in his speeches in the Acts of the Apostles and in his letters; though justification by grace through faith is often his prevailing insight, he never explains it exactly the same way twice. When one views Jesus' parable of the Pharisee and the tax collector as a drama with the same meaning, the possibilities of creative redundancy are even more apparent.

The whole church, of course, has more capacity for creative redundancy than a lone communicator. For example, a first-time attendee at a Willow Creek Seeker Service might come after several conversations with the friend who invited him. The first weekend he comes, he is exposed to several songs, a drama, and a sermon on grace; he buys a tape of the service on the way out, and swings by the Willow Creek bookstore for one of the recommended books or tapes on the subject of the day. He engages in several more conversations with his inviter, and with another fellow he meets at Willow Creek, and with still another fellow, also a seeker, at his workplace. He may attend several more weekend services in a series devoted to the grace theme. He may come to a forum where he can ask his question, or join a seekers group to work through it in the company of others.

8. They assimilate seekers *before* they believe.

More and more converts out of secularity report that their assimilation into the community of faith precedes their commitment or their discovery of faith. When I ask them, "When did you feel like you really belonged?" they often report that they felt that they belonged before they believed, and that feeling helped them believe. John Wesley observed this reality, and therefore encouraged seekers to join a Methodist class, and in three months a Methodist society, whether they yet experienced or believed anything. Wesley even saw the Eucharist as "a converting ordinance" and welcomed seekers to find the gracious presence at the table and altar.

Traditional evangelical churches more usually function by the opposite paradigm: Let people first get saved and profess faith, and then we will receive them into the fellowship circle. But increasing numbers of churches are rediscovering what Wesley knew—that the world is not stacked on the side of very many people finding saving faith, that occasional evangelical forays into the secular world do not greatly improve the odds, and that people are more likely to find faith through involvement within the Church than outside it, particularly involvement in its redemptive cells. Deiter Zander observes that, especially in the case of the Baby Buster generation, "We need to move the line of fellowship. People used to be allowed to cross the line into fellowship only after their conversion. Today, increasingly, we must first invite people into the fellowship so they can process what being in the fellowship is all about. So, at New Song, we created a fellowship that knew how to include seekers inside the circle."

9. They permit Christianity to become "contagious."

This reality introduces another principle: Lord Soper has long observed that the Christian faith is "more caught than taught." In part, the purpose of evangelistic ministry is to enable people to experience the contagion of the Christian faith. I have already alluded to several patterns that help produce this contagion: They are more likely to respond to original Christianity, in the receptive seasons of their lives, and from friends or relatives—who begin with their felt needs and questions, whose church meaningfully interprets the gospel in their language and cultural forms.

Furthermore, secular people are more likely to "catch" the faith inside the Church than outside it, more likely in a seeker service than a traditional service, more likely in small groups than in the larger church, more likely from a two-way conversation than a one-way presentation, more likely from lay Christians than from clergy, more likely from multiple experiences than from a single experience. Furthermore, they are more likely to catch faith by getting involved with the message, or a fellowship, or in service than by detached observing. Increasingly, churches see part of their mission as creating the kind of climate, worship, body life, conversation ministries, and involvement opportunities that permit seeking people to discover faith.

10. They invite an "experiment of faith."

Sam Shoemaker, decades ago, often invited people to conduct "an experiment of faith." This experiment meant living for a season, doing the things Christians do, as though Christianity is true; people could thereby discover for themselves whether Christianity is "self-authenticating." In a modification, Willow Creek invites people to connect "the wisdom of scripture" to one area of their life, like their marriage, for a season; people learn they can trust Scripture, so maybe they can trust God!

What Churches Discover When They "Go Apostolic"

We can now know more about the effective communication of Christianity to secular people than any other generation of faithful people have known since secularization began several centuries ago and, though they still number less than 2 percent of America's churches, more and more churches are now pioneering in apostolic mission in America's mission fields. I have been privileged to observe enough churches that have moved "from tradition to mission" that I can report five discoveries that these churches commonly experience.

1. The churches that decide to "major" in reaching unchurched pre-Christian people discover the reality of "prevenient grace"—that in every season God's spirit is preparing the hearts of some people to receive the gospel and experience saving grace. Therefore, the church discovers that it is always "harvesttime"; they can always find receptive people and groups in their ministry area.

For instance, a church in the Northeast decided to move "from tradition to mission." They prepared by starting a seeker service and by involving many of the members in new small groups, lay ministries, and evangelism training. A team of three lay people visited the home of a pre-Christian family. They asked, "Would you like to talk about what following Christ could mean in your lives, and the life of your family?" The family said they would be very interested. The rookie visitors exclaimed, "You would?" They report that God has been surprising them ever since!

2. Churches who begin to receive secular people into their ranks typically discover that these people bring their problems with them—often a different set of problems than the church is used to. The church also discovers that the grace of Christ is great enough for those problems too. The hundreds of churches adding 12 Step recovery ministries are especially discovering the power of Christ to liberate people from addictions to alcohol, drugs, food, sex, gambling, work, relationships, violence, and a number of other destructive compulsions.

3. Such churches discover the faith for themselves in new depth. When you spend part of your life explaining and interpreting the Christian faith to outsiders, you are driven into a deeper understanding of the faith's meaning than you could ever attain spending all of your time with Christians. This was, of course, the discovery of the original apostles. They became the normative theologians of the early Christian movement not only because most of them had spent three years with Jesus, but also because they had extended and interpreted the faith for some years to an unreached population.

4. Churches who "go apostolic" no longer miss the "home field advantage" of the Christendom period. Apostolic congregations are like the Notre Dame football team—who would rather play on the opponent's field because, as Coach Lou Holtz once explained, "It presents the greater challenge to our commitment, our character, our courage, and our community."

5. The new apostolic churches often experience a life, meaning, excitement, power, and contagion that more traditional churches seldom experience. In recent years, Skyline Wesleyan Church, in the San Diego area, has

targeted people with no Christian background. One Sunday, pastor John Maxwell was to baptize, by immersion, an athletic man into the faith. As the man reclined in the pool, with one of Maxwell's hands supporting him, Maxwell's other hand was poised above the man's forehead. The man looked at Maxwell's hand, over at his face, back at his hand, and gave Maxwell the "high five"! People across the congregation started "high-fiving" each other in a spontaneous celebration of new life in Christ.

Opportunity Everywhere (Yes, Everywhere)

I conclude with a claim that, once, I would have been too cautious to venture. We need "churches for the unchurched" virtually everywhere. When the Christian movement responds to this challenge, some new churches will be planted, some established churches will move "from tradition to mission," and some traditional churches will add seeker congregations to the options they offer people.

In a recent semester, I taught a section of our basic evangelism course at Asbury Theological Seminary. Some class members, bent on becoming chaplains for traditional churches, patiently endured my peculiar party line: "See your community as a mission field, and your church as a missionary church. Don't be content with mere church attendance or nominal Christianity, but only active discipleship. Start a worship service that begins where people are, speaks their language and celebrates the gospel through their music, done well enough to eliminate the 'cringe factor' and to free your people to engage and invite unchurched pre-Christians to their church."

Some students, however, responded to these ideas. An excellent second career student, Rick Baldwin, caught a vision exceeding my own. He proposed that Wilmore United Methodist church start a seeker service. He would organize a team of seminary students to help the church "reach Wilmore." As I heard his proposal and sensed Rick's Camelot-level vision, I cautiously encouraged him while harboring private doubts. Why the doubts?

Compared to most communities, Wilmore, Kentucky is not a hotbed of secular paganism. The most recent census reported a Wilmore population of 4,215, but some of us suspect that figure includes the animals and all known vegetation! If you toured Wilmore, you would observe Asbury College and Asbury Theological Seminary (both are Christian institutions in the Wesleyan-Holiness tradition), you would observe two traffic lights, Fitch's IGA Grocery, and a dozen shops—most still closed on Sunday. You would also notice a defunct railway station, several hundred houses, and little else! The town already supports at least eight churches!

I assumed, with almost everyone, that Wilmore was a clear exception to America becoming a mission field again. There was bound to be some truth to the local folk saying about "no sin within the Wilmore city limits!" However, Rick, his friends, and people from the local Missionary church surveyed Wilmore, and found more undiscipled people (about 1,800) than anyone had predicted. Their interviews revealed that Wilmore's unchurched people perceived the churches as irrelevant, money-hungry, and snobby and unfriendly; if they did go to a church—they would prefer Sunday morning at eleven.

Rick and his friends negotiated clearance to begin a "seeker service," in the spring of 1993, in the church's old sanctuary at eleven—the same time as the main traditional service in the newer, larger sanctuary. They brought a piano, two guitars, and drums into the old sanctuary. With the words on a screen, they sang songs like "Our God Is an Awesome God," "Shine, Jesus Shine," and "I Exalt Thee." Several seminary students took turns bringing the message. People were encouraged to dress casually.

The service did not always achieve the excellence the leaders wanted. Indeed, some of the leadership and style represented only a *partial* shift from revivalism toward a culturally relevant seeker service. The service struggled through that spring, summer, and fall of 1993, and into the early winter of 1994, averaging only about 40 in attendance. Late in this period, however, the students and several others were now befriending and inviting unchurched pre-Christian people in Wilmore! Twenty-two of the core attenders started visiting new attenders or became involved in lay ministries to unchurched people and new attenders.

In late winter of 1994 the service "took off," and by March through May of 1994 was averaging 200 in attendance (100 percent of the old sanctuary's capacity)! About one-third of the attenders in spring of 1994 were connected to the college, about one-third to the seminary, and the other third were unchurched people from Wilmore or from nearby Nicholasville. (Slicing the data differently, about half had attended the church before the contemporary service started; about half were new to the church.) By the end of May 1994, seven adults from the service had joined the church, and seven more had requested membership.

Alas, the eleven o'clock seeker service did not continue. Some of the church's leaders had criticized it when it was small and struggling; now some criticized it because it was growing, succeeding, and attracting several dozen people who otherwise might have attended the main service. A pastoral change provided leverage for "suspending" the seeker service for the summer of 1994. In the fall of 1994 the church established an alternative service at nine in the main sanctuary, but this "domesticated" version of Rick Baldwin's experiment is no longer seeker targeted; it is now an informal "contemporary" service for Christians. To its credit, youth, college students, and some other folks like it and attend it, but the season of Camelot is gone with the wind.

Nevertheless, Rick Baldwin and company had demonstrated a need, and a "market," in Wilmore (no less) for a culturally relevant church, featuring a contemporary service, with the apostolic vision to reach out and begin where secular seekers are. If there is need for an apostolic congregation in Wilmore, that need is everywhere! North America presents an unprecedented opportunity to the churches that care enough and dare enough to adapt to the emerging harvest. While most of us yet live, we will see a hundred thousand apostolic congregations across this land, with steady streams of new disciples entering their ranks, and Christianity will be a contagious movement in North America.

Selected Resources for Building an Apostolic Congregation

Contemporary Perspectives and Paradigms on the Local Church

Anderson, Leith. *A Church for the 21st Century: Bringing Change to Your Church to Meet the Challenges of a Changing Society.* Minneapolis, Minn.: Bethany House Publishers, 1992.

Frazee, Randy. *The Comeback Congregation: New Life for a Troubled Ministry.* Nashville: Abingdon Press, 1995.

Hybels, Lynne, and Bill. *Rediscovering Church: The Story and Vision of Willow Creek Community Church.* Grand Rapids, Mich.: Zondervan, 1995.

Kallestad, Walt, and Tim Wright. *The Mission-Driven Church.* A workbook and six cassettes, published by and available from The Community Church of Joy Book Shop, 16635 N. 51st Avenue, Glendale AZ 85306.

Mead, Loren B. *The Once and Future Church: Reinventing the Congregation for a New Mission Frontier.* Washington D.C.: The Alban Institute, 1991.

Mouw, Richard J. *Consulting the Faithful.* Grand Rapids, Mich.: Wm. B. Eerdmans, 1994.

Robinson, Martin. *A World Apart: Creating a Church for the Unchurched.* Tunbridge Wells, U.K.: Monarch Publications, 1992.

Roxburgh, Alan J. *Reaching A New Generation: Strategies for Tomorrow's Church.* Downers, Grove, Ill.: InterVarsity Press, 1993.

Schaller, Lyle. *Innovations in Ministry: Models for the Twenty-first Century.* Nashville: Abingdon Press, 1994.

———. *The Seven-Day-A-Week Church.* Nashville: Abingdon Press, 1992.

Slaughter, Michael. *Beyond Playing Church: A Christ-Centered Environment for Church Renewal.* Anderson, Ind.: Bristol House, 1994.

Sweet, Leonard. *FaithQuakes*. Nashville: Abingdon Press, 1994.

Towns, Elmer L. *An Inside Look at Ten of Today's Most Innovative Churches*. Ventura, Calif.: Regal Books, 1990.

Warren, Rick. *The Purpose-Driven Church*. Grand Rapids, Mich.: Zondervan, 1995.

Contemporary Services and Seeker Services

Benedict, Daniel, and Craig Kennet Miller. *Contemporary Worship for the 21st Century: Worship or Evangelism?* Nashville: Discipleship Resources, 1994.

Dobson, Ed. *Starting a Seeker Sensitive Service: How Traditional Churches Can Reach the Unchurched*. Grand Rapids, Mich.: Zondervan, 1993.

Warren, Rick. "How to Build a Seeker Sensitive Service" (2 tapes).

———. "Communicating to Change Lives" (on preaching—2 tapes).

———. "Saddleback Church Growth Lectures" (Rick Warren's tapes are available from: The Encouraging Word, Box 6080-388, Mission Viejo CA 92690).

Wright, Timothy. *A Community of Joy: How to Create Contemporary Worship*. Nashville: Abingdon Press, 1994.

The most widely used suppliers of contemporary Christian music include:

- **Integrity's Hosanna Music,** P.O. Box Z, Mobile AL 36616. Tel. (800) 239-7000.
- **The Vineyard,** Psalmist Resources, 94820 East Watson Road, St. Louis MO 63126. Tel. (314) 842-6161.
- **Maranatha Music Net,** P.O. Box 1396, Costa Mesa CA 92628. Tel. (800) 245-7664.
- **Christian Copyright Licensing, Inc.,** 6130 NE 78th Court, Suite C11, Portland OR 97216-2853. Tel. (800) 234-2446.
  Their blanket license covers most major religious music publishers. It allows a congregation to print the words to songs in the worship bulletin or project the words on a screen. Call or write for fees and information.

Evangelism and Church Growth

Arn, Win, and Charles Arn. *The Master's Plan for Making Disciples*. Pasadena, Calif.: Church Growth Press, 1982.

Barna, George. *Evangelism That Works*. Ventura, Calif.: Regal Books, 1995.

Green, Michael. *Evangelism Through the Local Church*. Nashville: Thomas Nelson, 1990.

Hunter, George G., III. *How to Reach Secular People.* Nashville: Abingdon Press, 1992.

_____. *To Spread the Power: Church Growth in the Wesleyan Spirit.* Nashville: Abingdon Press, 1987.

Hybels, Bill, and Mark Mittelberg. *Becoming a Contagious Christian.* Grand Rapids, Mich.: Zondervan, 1994.

Kallestad, Walt, and Tim Wright. *Reaching the Unchurched: Creating the Vision, Planning to Grow.* Minneapolis: Augsburg Fortress, 1994. A four-session "video workshop" for a local church's planning committee. In four parts: (1) Creating a Vision, (2) Knowing the Parts, (3) Reaching the Audience, (4) Planning for Growth. Includes handouts that "may be reproduced for local use."

McGavran, Donald A. *Understanding Church Growth,* 3rd ed. Grand Rapids, Mich.: Eerdmans, 1990.

Mathison, John Ed. *Tried and True: Eleven Principles of Church Growth from Frazer Memorial United Methodist Church.* Nashville: Discipleship Resources, 1992.

Mittelberg, Mark, Lee Strobel, and Bill Hybels. *Becoming a Contagious Christian Evangelism Seminar.* Grand Rapids, Mich.: Zondervan, 1995. The kit includes participant's guide, leader's guide, and video of dramas.

Sjogren, Steve. *Conspiracy of Kindness.* Ann Arbor, Mich.: Servant Publications, 1993.

Strobel, Lee. *Inside the Mind of Unchurched Harry and Mary.* Grand Rapids, Mich.: Zondervan, 1993.

Wright, Tim. *Unfinished Evangelism: More Than Getting Them in the Door.* Minneapolis, Minn.: Augsburg Fortress, 1995.

Lay Ministries

Bugbee, Bruce, Don Cousins, and Bill Hybels. *NetWork: The Right People . . . In the Right Places . . . For the Right Reasons.* Grand Rapids, Mich.: Zondervan, 1994.

This excellent $155 kit features Willow Creek's complete seminar for helping people discover their spiritual gifts, passion, and personal style—as a means to the end of getting people involved in the right ministries for them. The kit contains (1) a participant's guide, (2) an implementation guide, (3) a consultant's guide, (4) a leader's guide, and (5) two training videos.

Galloway, Dale E. *Ministry Skills for Small Group Leaders.* A workbook with 52 Training Lessons and eight cassettes. Available from New Hope Community Church's book shop, 11731 S.E. Stevens Road, Portland OR 97266. Tel. (503) 659-5683.

This workbook, which presents the 52 lessons that train New Hope's lay pastors, is one good example of what is possible in preparing laity for pastoral care. The lessons cover basic insights in eight different units:

- **Bible:** Knowing your Bible and how to use it
- **Christian Leadership:** Principles for spiritual leadership
- **Counseling:** Basic skills in personal and biblical counseling
- **Evangelism and Discipleship:** Outreach and spiritual growth
- **Lay Pastor Skills:** Principles for providing pastoral care
- **Personal Management:** Training for effective living
- **Small Group Skills:** Basic skills for leading a small group
- **Theology:** Knowing the basic beliefs of the Christian faith

The unit on lay pastoral skills includes lessons on: Visitation in the Home, Visiting the Sick and Hospitalized, Ministry to Crisis Needs, Helping People Deal with Grief and Loss, How to Pray for Healing, and The Ministry of Caring. More specifically, the lesson on Helping People Deal with Grief and Loss features biblical insights on grief and loss, and then introduces the common phases of grief [from Elisabeth Kübler-Ross, *On Death and Dying* (New York: Macmillan, 1993)], with suggestions for pastoring at each stage from Wayne Oates' *Pastoral Care and Counseling in Grief and Separation* (Minneapolis, Minn.: Augsburg Fortress, 1976). New Hope's lay pastors are also mentored by a district pastor and take weekly ongoing training at the church.

Kraemer, Hendrick. *A Theology of the Laity.* Louisville, Ky.: Westminster Press, 1958.

Ogden, Greg. *The New Reformation: Returning the Ministry to the People of God.* Grand Rapids, Mich.: Zondervan, 1990.

Snyder, Howard. *Liberating the Church.* Downers Grove, Ill.: InterVarsity Press, 1983.

Steinbron, Melvin J. *Can the Pastor Do It Alone? A Model for Preparing Lay People for Lay Pastoring.* Ventura, Calif.: Regal Books, 1987.

Tillapaugh, Frank. *Unleashing the Church.* Ventura, Calif.: Regal Books, 1992.

Trueblood, Elton. *The Incendiary Fellowship.* New York: Harper and Row, 1967.

Warren, Rick. "How to Turn an Audience into an Army" (tape).

———. "CLASS 301: Discovering MY SHAPE" curriculum. (Tapes available from: The Encouraging Word, Box 6080-388, Mission Viejo CA 92690.)

Recovery Ministries

Baker, John. "Saddleback's Recovery Program"—6 booklets published locally by Saddleback Valley Community Church, n.d. Available from:

The Encouraging Word
Box 6080-388
Mission Viejo, CA 92690

Galloway, Dale E. "New Life Victorious" (Spiritual Recovery Program), section 4 in Dale Galloway, *7 Days-A-Week Church: How To Build Multi-Need Meeting Ministries*. Portland, Ore.: New Hope Community Church, 1994.

Dale Galloway's "New Life Victorious" manual is the best comprehensive introduction I have seen to what a local church is actually doing, why, and how, in recovery ministries. This manual is merely one of twenty-one manuals in this three-ring volume on New Hope's ministries. Other manuals within this collection introduce their ministries to children, youth, singles, young adults, adults, men, women, and senior adults; to their ministries around marriage—premarital counseling, separation survival, divorce recovery, premarital counseling before remarriage, and remarrieds ministry; to their ministries to visitors, new members, developing disciples, and deployed volunteers in tasks and ministries; to New Hope's ministries around grief and loss recovery, and prayer and healing ministries. The manual on worship and music is also an outstanding resource for churches wanting to move into more contemporary and culturally relevant worship experiences for seekers and believers.

Available from New Hope Community Church's bookstore, 11731 S.E. Stevens Road, Portland OR 97266. Tel. 1-800-935-4673.

Miller, J. Keith. *A Hunger for Healing: The Twelve Steps as a Classic Model for Christian Spiritual Growth*. San Francisco: HarperCollins, 1991.

Morris, Bill. *The Complete Handbook for Recovery Ministry in the Church: A Practical Guide to Establishing Recovery Support Groups within Your Church*. Nashville: Thomas Nelson, 1993. (Includes an excellent bibliography.)

Twelve Steps and Twelve Traditions. New York: Alcoholics Anonymous World Services Inc., 1952.

Secularization and Postmodernity

Allen, Diogenes. *Christian Belief in a Postmodern World: The Full Wealth of Conviction*. Louisville, Ky.: Westminster/John Knox Press, 1989.

Berger, Peter L. *A Rumor of Angels: Modern Society and the Rediscovery of the Supernatural*. Rev. ed. New York: Anchor Books/Doubleday, 1990.

Bibby, Reginald. *Fragmented Gods: The Poverty and Potential of Religion in Canada*. Toronto: Irwin Publishing, 1987.

Chadwick, Owen. *The Secularization of the European Mind in the Nineteenth Century*. London: Cambridge University Press, 1985.

Dyrness, William. *How Does America Hear the Gospel?* Grand Rapids, Mich.: Eerdmans, 1989.

Newbigin, Lesslie. *Foolishness to the Greeks: The Gospel and Western Culture*. Grand Rapids, Mich.: Eerdmans, 1986.

_____. *The Gospel in a Pluralist Society*. Grand Rapids, Mich.: Eerdmans, 1989.

Small Groups

Arnold, Jeffrey. *The Big Book On Small Groups*. Downers Grove, Ill.: InterVarsity Press, 1992.

Coleman, Lyman. *Basic Training for Small Group Leaders*. Littleton, Colo.: Serendipity House, 1992.

Donahue, Bill. *Willow Creek Small Groups: Leadership Handbook*. South Barrington, Ill.: Willow Creek Community Church, 1994.

Galloway, Dale E. *20/20 Vision: How To Create a Successful Church*. Rev. ed. Portland, Ore.: Scott Publishing Company, 1993.

George, Carl. *Prepare Your Church for the Future*. Tarrytown, N.Y.: Fleming H. Revell Company, 1991.

Griffin, Em. *Getting Together: A Guide for Good Groups*. Downers Grove, Ill.: InterVarsity Press, 1982.

Neighbor, Ralph W., Jr. *Where Do We Go From Here?* Houston, Tex.: Touch Publications, 1990.

Scazzero, Peter. *Introducing Jesus: Starting an Investigative Bible Study for Seekers*. Downers Grove, Ill.: InterVarsity Press, 1991.

Sorensen, Paul, and Tim Hedrick. *Small Group Leader's Training Manual*. A workbook, published by and available from The Community Church of Joy Book Shop, 16635 N. 51st Avenue, Glendale AZ 85306.

Wuthnow, Robert. *Sharing the Journey: Support Groups and America's New Quest for Community*. New York: MacMillan Press, 1994.

Notes

1. The Rebirth of the Apostolic Congregation

1. See my fuller treatment of the history of secularization, and a profile of secular people, in George G. Hunter III, *How to Reach Secular People* (Nashville: Abingdon Press, 1992), introduction and chapters 1-2.

2. By 1988, 18 percent of America's people reported no religious training. I received these statistics in a November 15, 1994 telephone conversation with George Gallup, Jr. (Gallup reported that the 1952 and 1965 data were published in *The Catholic Digest*. The 1978 and 1988 data were reported in Gallup's book *The Unchurched American*.) In our conversation, Dr. Gallup reported that the level of religious knowledge has declined, that the religious transference from generation to generation is getting weaker and weaker. As a consequence, he says, most Americans do not know what they believe, or why. Indeed, most professing Christians cannot explain, much less defend, their faith. Gallup regards the average Christian's lack of preparedness as a greater threat to the future of Christianity than the external phenomenon of secularization.

Gallup's survey data probably do not fully reflect the extent to which the secularization of American minds continues; the move from 17 percent reporting no religious training in 1978 to 18 percent in 1988 is not as precipitous as the somewhat earlier drops. This apparent leveling off may be due to the tendencies of many people today to misrepresent the facts in "self reporting" surveys; i.e., many people now report how they like to think of themselves (or how they want the interviewer to think of them). For example, 15 percent more people said they voted in the 1992 presidential election than actually voted! In the 1994 congressional elections, 39 percent of the eligible registered voters actually voted; a random sampling revealed that 52 percent said they voted! So, the real 1988 figure probably should have been closer to 25 percent without religious training.

Sociologist Kirk Hadaway has observed the same problem regarding self-reported church attendance surveys. While self-reported church attendance remains at about 42 percent, Hadaway's research in "typical" Ohio counties revealed that only about 20 percent of the population actually attend on a typical Sunday. See C. Kirk Hadaway, Penny Long Marler, and Mark Chaves, "What the Polls Don't Show: A Closer Look At U.S. Church Attendance," in *American Sociological Review* (December, 1993). The authors contend that the gap between those who go and those who report that they go, "may have expanded over the last several decades."

I contend that the numbers of people without any religious training in their background has also increased more than the (self-reported) Gallup data suggests. One reason behind this claim is the universal experience of churches with a long-term apostolic orientation; they all meet an increasing number of people with no Christian memory. Another reason can be inferred from Gallup's data from the 1960s and 1970s: The first major drop-off in the number of people receiving religious training (and in other indicators of Christian influence upon people) occurred in the 1960s and early 1970s. That generation's children, now adults, are even less likely to provide for religious training for their children—which would accelerate the trend away from religious training once again.

3. *Newsweek* (November 28, 1994): 52-54.

4. Ibid., 54.

5. Ibid., 53.

6. Ibid., 53.

7. For two excellent treatments of the Enlightenment and Modernity, see Diogenes Allen, *Christian Belief in a Postmodern World: The Full Wealth of Conviction* (Louisville: Westminster/John Knox Press, 1989) and Stephen Toulmin, *Cosmopolis: The Hidden Agenda of Modernity* (New York: Free Press, 1990).

8. Toulmin, *The Hidden Agenda of Modernity*. To build rational societies that functioned like clockwork was, Toulmin explains, "the hidden agenda of Modernity."

9. David Burnett explains humanity's varied approaches to the supernatural, including the postmodern recovery of a sense of the supernatural, in two excellent books—*Unearthly Powers* (Nashville: Thomas Nelson Publishers, 1992) and *Clash of Worlds* (Nashville: Thomas Nelson Publishers, 1992). He demonstrates, for instance, that the New Age movement is a symptom of postmodern people's "flight from secularism," and how it draws (selectively) from pre-Christian Saxon, Celtic, and other ancient religions—and even from Shamanism, Witchcraft, and Satanism, as well as from Eastern religions and from modern science and psychology.

10. For example, Ron Johnson—director of evangelism for the Georgia state convention of the Southern Baptist Church, estimates that 20 percent of their members are trained in personal evangelism, but only 1 percent actually do it in a typical year.

11. When Christians have said "yes," I have asked "How do you go about that?" I have learned a great deal from the Christians who actually do it!

12. Lee Strobel, *Inside the Mind of Unchurched Harry and Mary* (Grand Rapids, Mich.: Zondervan, 1993), 162-63. I have observed that some people, especially people "in process," do not fit one of Strobel's types perfectly. For instance, as churches have failed to adapt to the music and changing culture of the "Baby Buster" generation, many adults who were once teenage Christians within our ranks are now unchurched Christians. Again, many people who are unchurched Christians today will one day be unchurched non-Christians—because faith is best sustained within the fellowship of faith. We find other people are "somewhere between" two of the types as, for example, the Christians who are nominally churched.

13. The terms "secular people" and "unchurched non-Christians" are not fully synonymous or overlapping. For example, I meet (fairly often) non-Christians who are nominal church members but are essentially secular, i.e., they have not been substantially influenced by the Christian faith and do not really know what Christianity means; it has, for whatever reasons, washed past them. Furthermore, I occasionally meet unchurched non-Christians who are not secular, i.e., they have a Christian memory, background, and vocabulary. Nevertheless, so many unchurched non-Christians are secular people that the terms may virtually be used interchangeably, and I have found that to talk about "unchurched non-Christians" as well as "secular people" helps church leaders to understand and own our apostolic challenge and opportunity.

14. I began researching three of this book's themes—goals for people, cultural relevance, and communication with secular people—long before visiting these nine churches; some of the insights in chapters 2, 3, and 6 were, therefore, more confirmed than learned from these congregations. But the profile of "apostolic congregations" in this chapter, and the insights on small groups and lay ministries in chapters 4 and 5 were substantially learned from these churches.

15. Many people, even writers, assume that a problem has a single cause, and a solution requires a single intervention. However, we know from the research base of Organization Development that reality in organizations is always more complex than people usually

assume. Consequently, this project identifies some of the multiple interventions that many congregations will have to engage in to become contagious and effective in outreach.

16. The apostolic tradition tells us that most of the original apostles devoted years to extending Christianity and interpreting the gospel to one or more distinct unreached populations. For example, Peter took the gospel to Asia Minor, Babylon, and Rome. Thomas planted the faith in South India; Philip took it to other parts of Asia and to Athens; James (the brother of John) was the apostle to Spain, and Bartholomew to India; Jude and Simon the Zealot formed one of the early Christian movement's many "apostolic teams" and took the faith to Persia. See George G. Hunter III, *How to Reach Secular People* (Nashville: Abingdon Press, 1992), 108-11; and also William Barclay, *The Master's Men* (Nashville: Abingdon Press, 1959).

17. This feature of communicating the apostolic message also served this project as a criterion for excluding some churches from this study. I excluded several churches that have deviated enough from the apostles' doctrines (and from their theological tradition) to confuse Christianity with "prosperity gospel," civil religion, or even super-patriotism. I regarded data from such churches as useless to this project.

18. I was tempted to demonstrate the precedents for today's apostolic churches from all three Reformation expressions and from several Third World fields, but decided to confine the focus on Reformation precedents to John Wesley's eighteenth-century Methodist movement (because I know it best) and to confine the contemporary focus to North America. I judged that extensive Reformation and global material would detract from the mission of this project.

19. I would not pretend that the apostolic congregations from which I draw insight are "perfect" churches to copy at all points. When they launched out, in the 1970s, to become churches for reaching unchurched pre-Christian people, they lacked precedents and models, and most of them even lacked the support of their denominations. So, as Nancy Beach from Willow Creek confesses, they made it up as they went along and they made mistakes along the way. Each of these churches has problems today—but I prefer the kind of problems they have to the kind I find in more traditional congregations!

20. Michael Slaughter, *Beyond Playing Church: A Christ-Centered Environment for Church Renewal* (Anderson, Ind.: Bristol House, 1994), 69.

21. Bruce Larson and Ralph Osborne, *The Emerging Church* (Waco, Tex.: Word Books, 1970).

22. I am not suggesting that Christians must experience all ten of these distinctives of the apostolic church before they can engage in effective outreach. The extent of my research does not permit me to prescribe "how many" of the ten are necessary, or "which ones," but I can speculate. I have not interviewed many people doing outreach who were not motivated by compassion; that is probably an essential. I have interviewed a fair number who did not particularly refer to the Great Commission; there are other biblical or theological themes that also impel people to reach out. Small groups and pastoral care are similar enough experiences that many people are doing outreach from the experience of one or the other. I can speculate that: (1) Each distinctive a church adds should increase its outreach effectiveness, and (2) The more of these a person experiences, the more likely he or she will engage in outreach, and the more of these that a church puts in place, the more "apostolic" it will be.

2. What People Can Become

1. Loren B. Mead, *The Once and Future Church: Reinventing the Congregation for a New Mission Frontier* (Washington D.C.: The Alban Institute, 1991), 22.

2. See Tatiana Goricheva, *Talking About God Is Dangerous* (New York: Crossroads, 1986), 17.

3. James Russell Lowell, "The Present Crisis" in *The Complete Poetical Works of James Russell Lowell* (Boston: Houghton Mifflin, 1925), 67.

4. Stephen C. Neill, "Conversion," *Scottish Journal of Theology*, vol. 3 (1950).

3. A Case for the Culturally Relevant Congregation

1. The requirement of circumcision is fortunate, because it illustrates, metaphorically, that changing one's culture is not a superficial act, like changing one jacket for another, because a person's basic identity is involved. The circumcision metaphor also illustrates that a person feels vulnerable when considering culture change.

2. This principle of indigenousness was to become one of Christianity's towering differences with Islam. Muslims believe that the Koran cannot really be translated, that its full meaning can be apprehended only within the original Arabic language and culture. But Christians have discovered that the Christian scriptures can be translated into any tongue on earth, and that Christianity's essential meaning can be apprehended through any culture.

3. See Martin Robinson, *A World Apart: Creating a Church for the Unchurched* (Tunbridge Wells, U.K.: Monarch Publications, 1992), 37. Chapter 2, "Secularization and the Contemporary Church," is especially helpful.

4. Robinson, *A World Apart*, 37.

5. C. Peter Wagner, *Church Growth and the Whole Gospel: A Biblical Mandate* (San Francisco: Harper & Row, 1981), 177-78.

6. David Burnett, *Clash of Worlds* (Nashville: Thomas Nelson Publishers, 1992). See especially chapter 13, "The Biblical Worldview."

7. See *The Willowbank Report—Gospel and Culture*, Lausanne Occasional Paper no. 2 (1978), 13.

8. See Kenneth Scott Latourette, *A History of Christianity, Volume 2* (New York: Harper & Row, 1953), 721, 732.

9. John Wesley, "The Character of a Methodist," *The Works of John Wesley, Volume 8* (Grand Rapids, Mich.: Baker Book House), 340.

10. Lyle Schaller, "When, How, & Why to *Change* Your Worship Service," *Circuit Rider*, vol. 18, no. 10 (December 1994/January 1995): 10.

11. Walther P. Kallestad, "Entertainment Evangelism," *The Lutheran* (May 23, 1990): 17.

12. *Circuit Rider*, vol. 18, no. 10 (December 1994/January 1995).

13. Don E. Saliers, "Our Liturgical Dilemma," *Circuit Rider*, vol. 18, no. 10 (December 1994/January 1995): 4-6.

14. "Big-band Fan Turns Missionary to Metal Heads," *Christianity Today* (February 10, 1992): 10-11.

4. How Small Groups Shape an Apostolic People

1. From this verse Dale Galloway, of the New Hope Community Church in Portland recommends *20/20 Vision* for churches wanting to reach people and grow. See Dale E. Galloway, *20/20 Vision: How to Create a Successful Church* (Portland, Ore.: Scott Publishing Company, 1986, revised 1993).

2. I have shown the biblical/early church foundation for the church growth strategy called "the multiplication of units" in chapter 5 of George G. Hunter III, *To Spread the Power: Church Growth in the Wesleyan Spirit* (Nashville: Abingdon Press, 1987), 109-29.

3. For a much more thorough account of early Christianity's formation—in its social and cultural context—see Wayne A. Meeks, "The Formation of the Ekklesia," *The First Urban Christians: The Social World of the Apostle Paul*, chapter 3 (New Haven, Conn.: Yale University Press, 1983).

4. Hunter, *To Spread the Power*, 125. Emphasis added.

5. Kenneth Scott Latourette. *A History of Christianity, Volume II: Reformation to the Present* (New York: Harper and Row, 1953), 894-97.

6. Early Methodism developed as a lay apostolic and renewal order within the Church of England, so the Methodist Societies, which met in chapels, were (more or less) loyal to the

Church of England. Following Wesley's death, Methodism separated from the Church of England—with some "push" from the Anglicans! The societies thus became "churches."

7. Hunter, *To Spread the Power*, 58. See chapters 2 and 5 for more insight on Wesley's use of the classes within his apostolic strategy.

8. Dale E. Galloway, *20/20 Vision: How to Create a Successful Church*, 126.

9. Two types of groups, however, need to be "closed" once their membership is constituted: grief recovery groups and marital reconciliation groups.

10. New Hope gives its extensive network of lay pastors several time options for the ongoing weekly training: 8:15 A.M. and 5:15 P.M. on Sundays, and 9:30 A.M. and 5:30 P.M. on Wednesdays.

11. Galloway, *20/20 Vision*, 155.

12. Ibid., 150.

13. I realize that Willow Creek, in recent years, has changed the seventh step to a stewardship step, but I do not applaud the "revised standard version" of their seven-step strategy. While I realize that a convert's wallet is usually the last part of his or her anatomy to be converted, I believe that stewardship sensitizing needs to be introduced earlier in the process (Saddleback does it at "second base"), I believe that its prominence at the end could reinforce any latent fears in converts out of secularity that "all they really wanted, after all, was my money," and I believe that this change butchers the full circle elegance of their original version of the strategy.

14. David L. Olsson, *Willow Creek Community Church Church Leaders Handbook*, Second Edition (South Barrington, Ill.: Willow Creek Association, 1993), 69. © 1993 Willow Creek Association. Reprinted with permission.

15. *Church Leaders Handbook*, 70.

16. Ibid., 71.

17. *Willow Creek Small Groups Leadership Handbook* (Willow Creek Community Church, 1994), 7. © 1994 Willow Creek Community Church. Reprinted with permission.

18. *Willow Creek Small Groups Leadership Handbook*, 3.

19. Bob and Betty Jacks with Ron Wormser, Sr., *Your Home a Lighthouse* (Colorado Springs, Colo.: NavPress, 1986). Denise Theetge leads this ministry at Saddleback, in cooperation with Navigators. For information, she can be reached at Saddleback Church, 23456 Madera, Suite 100, Mission Viejo, CA 92691. Tel. (714) 581-9100 extension 140. Fax (714) 581-7614.

20. Excerpt from "Lift High the Cross" by George McLeod, as printed in *Lighthouse: A Training Seminar on Hosting and Leading Home or Office Evangelistic Bible Studies*, a training resource used by Saddleback Valley Community Church.

21. Saddleback defines "insanity," for the people in their recovery ministries, as "Doing the same thing over and over again, each time expecting a different result!"

22. The "Serenity Prayer," usually attributed to Reinhold Niebuhr, from a brochure distributed by Saddleback Valley Community Church.

23. A group for adults who were raised in a dysfunctional family, for finding how the lost childhood issues are affecting present relationships with God, others, and self.

24. A group to help people who are dependent upon another person for their happiness, who feel responsible for another's happiness by doing for them what they can and should be doing for themselves, and to find new healthy ways to take care of their own needs.

25. "A group to encourage people to get in touch with repressed, numbed emotions and feelings, so resolution can come and freedom is found from fear, anxiety, and depression."

26. "To help people learn boundaries and to make decisions to make their lives become manageable by finding the real problem that is causing the repeated crisis."

27. Excerpt from poem by Hallmark's Amanda Bradley.

28. *Willow Creek Community Church Church Leaders Handbook*, 79.

29. Ibid., 85.

30. Galloway's "New Life Victorious" manual is a good introduction to what a local church is actually doing, and why, and how, in recovery ministries. Indeed, I strongly recommend the three-ring volume *Dale Galloway's 7 Days-a-Week Church: How to Build Multi-Need Meeting Ministries*, in which this resource is merely 1 of 21 manuals on New Hope's ministries.

31. See Flavil R. Yeakley, Jr., *The Discipling Dilemma: A Study of the Discipling Movement Among Churches of Christ* (Nashville: Gospel Advocate Company, 1988).

32. See Robert Wuthnow, *Sharing the Journey: Support Groups and America's New Quest for Community* (New York: Free Press, 1994).

33. *Sharing the Journey*, 78.

34. Ibid., 230-31.

35. Ibid., 350-51.

36. Wuthnow, in *Sharing the Journey*, 251-55, sees the tendency of groups to become "insular," so he sees value in group members participating in church programs and activities, church friendships, teaching, and worship services. He also reports, positively, that group members who report their faith having deepened seem to have a "less privatized" faith and to have a more positive attitude toward churches. But all of that falls considerably on the "domesticated" side of the large "celebration" we find in apostolic churches.

37. *Sharing the Journey*, 229.

38. Ibid., 278.

39. Ibid., 246.

40. Ibid.

41. Steve Sjogren, *Conspiracy of Kindness* (Ann Arbor, Mich.: Servant Publications, 1993), 190-91. A later chapter will unpack the distinctive "service evangelism" approach that characterizes this important pioneering congregation.

5. How Lay Ministry Advances the Christian Movement

1. Kenneth Scott Latourette, *A History of Christianity, Volume II: Reformation to the Present* (New York: Harper and Row, 1953), 713-14. Copyright 1953 by Harper & Brothers, renewed © 1981 by Wilma E. Hogg, Errol Hollowel and Alan Hollowel. Revised edition copyright © 1975 by Harper & Row, Publishers, Inc. Reprinted by permission of Harper Collins Publishers, Inc.

2. See Greg Ogden, *The New Reformation: Returning the Ministry to the People of God* (Grand Rapids, Mich.: Zondervan Publishing House, 1990).

3. John Ed Mathison, *Every Member in Ministry* (Nashville: Discipleship Resources, 1988), 21-22.

4. Ibid., 32.

5. Bruce Bugbee, Don Cousins, and Bill Hybels, *Network: The Right People . . . In the Right Places . . . For the Right Reasons* (Grand Rapids, Mich.: Zondervan Publishing House, 1994), 230.

6. David L. Olsson, *Willow Creek Community Church Church Leader's Handbook,* Second Edition (South Barrington, Ill.: Willow Creek Association, 1993), 118.

7. Excerpts from audiotapes of a #301 Seminar on Ministry, taught by Rick Warren, at Saddleback Valley Community Church.

8. Excerpts from an outline used by Saddleback.

9. Excerpts from *Saddleback Church Lay Pastor Institute* training resource.

10. Melvin J. Steinbron. *Can the Pastor Do It Alone? A Model for Preparing Lay People for Lay Pastoring* (Ventura, Calif.: Regal Books, 1987).

11. Ibid., 63. Chapter 5 delineates these four roles.

12. Michael Slaughter, *Beyond Playing Church: A Christ-Centered Environment for Church Renewal* (Anderson, Ind.: Bristol House, 1994), 133.

13. Steve Sjogren, *Conspiracy of Kindness* (Ann Arbor, Mich.: Servant Publications, 1993), 17-18.

14. Ibid., chapter 3.

15. Ibid., chapter 5.

6. How Apostolic Churches Reach Secular People

1. David J. Bosch, *Transforming Mission: Paradigm Shifts in Theology of Mission* (Maryknoll, N.Y.: Orbis Books, 1991), 277.

2. For a full explanation of Wesley's "Ordo Salutis" see George G. Hunter III, *To Spread the Power: Church Growth in the Wesleyan Spirit* (Nashville: Abingdon Press, 1987), chapter 2, especially 56-59.

3. David L. Olsson, *Willow Creek Community Church Church Leaders' Handbook*, Second Edition (South Barrington, Ill.: Willow Creek Association, 1993), 179.

4. Cliffe Knechtle, *Give Me An Answer* (Downers Grove, Ill.: InterVarsity, 1986).

5. George G. Hunter III, *How to Reach Secular People* (Nashville: Abingdon Press, 1992), 113-17.

6. Thomas A. Wolf, "Oikos Evangelism: Key to the Future," in *Future Church*, Ralph W. Neighbor, compiler (Nashville: Broadman Press, 1980), 153-54, 166.

7. See Paul G. Hiebert, "The Flaw of the Excluded Middle," in *Missiology: An International Review*, vol. X, no. 1 (January, 1982): 35-47. See also Bryant Myers, "The Excluded Middle," in *MARC Newsletter*, Number 91-2 (June 1991): 3-4.

8. Paul G. Hiebert, "The Flaw of the Excluded Middle," 45.

9. Ibid.

10. S. Bryant Myers, "The Excluded Middle," 3.

11. Paul G. Hiebert, "The Flaw of the Excluded Middle," 46.

Index